A Garland Series

Accounting History and th

A thirty-eight-volume facsimile series

evelopment of a Profession

Edited by Richard P. Brief, NEW YORK UNIVERSITY

Some Early Contributions to the Study of Audit Judgment

Edited by Robert H. Ashton

GARLAND PUBLISHING, INC.
NEW YORK & LONDON   1984

For a complete list of the titles in this series
see the final pages of this volume.

The editor gratefully acknowledges the permission of the
following to reprint material in this book: The American
Institute of Certified Public Accountants, Kenneth W. Stringer,
Gary L. Holstrum, William R. Kinney, and Blaine R. Ritts.

Library of Congress Cataloging in Publication Data
Main entry under title:

Some early contributions to the study of audit judgment.

(Accounting history and the development of a profession)
1. Auditing—History—Addresses, essays, lectures.
I. Ashton, Robert H.   II. Series.
HF5667.S636   1984   657'.45'09   83-49436
ISBN 0-8240-6303-1 (alk. paper)

The volumes in this series are printed on
acid-free, 250-year-life paper.

Printed in the United States of America

Contents

Introduction

Pressures from competition, litigation and business sophistication have caused independent auditors to seek new ways of improving the effectiveness and efficiency of their services. This has led to a growing recognition that audit evidence is collected and evaluated under conditions of uncertainty, and that audit decisions are based on imperfect and incomplete information. One consequence has been a heightened awareness of the crucial role that professional judgment plays in audit decision making.

This awareness has led to an increased emphasis on research that attempts to understand, evaluate and improve audit decision making. Recent developments in the field of cognitive psychology have made such research feasible. Psychologists have made substantial progress toward understanding the nature and limitations of individual judgment, including the professional judgment of experts in their fields of specialization. During the past decade, much of this research has been extended by auditing researchers to auditing decision contexts, and it has received substantial attention from researchers and practitioners interested in improving audit decision making.*

It is less well-known, however, that some noteworthy contributions to the study of audit judgment were made in the two decades prior to the 1970s. This anthology contains five such contributions which are either previously unpublished, out-of-print, or otherwise not widely appreciated.

The first selection, by Mautz (1959), argues for the importance of studying audit judgment, and it contains a call for research. The following three selections—Committee on Auditing Procedure (1955), Stringer (1959), and Kinney and Ritts (1973)—report actual studies of audit judgment, based on experiments designed to represent some of the essential features of audit decision settings. The

---

*The research in auditing contexts is reviewed and analyzed in Robert H. Ashton, *Research in Audit Decision Making: Rationale, Evidence, and Implications*, Research Monograph No. 6 (Canadian Certified General Accountants' Research Foundation, 1983).

basic outcome of these three studies is the demonstration of wide variations across auditors in planning the audit program and in judgmentally selecting sample sizes. The final item, by Brown (1962), proposes a simple technique for quantifying the evaluation of internal controls. This technique may be considered a precursor to today's "structured decision aids," the usefulness of which is often suggested as one implication of research in audit judgment.

Robert H. Ashton
New York City
November 1983

By R. K. Mautz

Evidence, Judgment, and the Auditor's Opinion

Four distinct steps are listed as essential to the formation of sound judgment by an auditor with respect to propositions asserted in financial statements:

1. Recognition of the proposition

2. Collection of pertinent evidence

3. Evaluation of the evidence

4. Formation of an opinion as to the conformity of the proposition with events as the auditor understands them

The auditor's opinion on financial statements taken as a whole is shown to be the result of a complex series of subsidiary judgments in which these four steps are followed.

THE independent auditor's opinion has been described in a variety of ways. Perhaps the best known description is that given by Saul Levy who terms it an expert, independent, informed, technical, and candid opinion.[1] As Mr. Levy points out, these important characteristics are indicative of the nature of an independent auditor's work and suggest the extent of his legal responsibility. From

[1] Levy, Saul, *Accountants' Legal Responsibility*, American Institute of CPAs, 1954, p. 7.

another point of view, other characteristics might be equally significant. To understand fully the independent auditor's problem of judgment formation and his use of evidence, for example, it must be recognized that an audit report is a composite and a complex opinion as well as one possessing the significant attributes mentioned by Mr. Levy.

Complexity of data to be considered

It is a composite opinion because it is based upon and made up of a host of subsidiary opinions or judgments. The financial statements which the independent auditor examines and about which he expresses his opinion are themselves composed of a large number of individual propositions on which he must make judgments and form opinions. The amount of cash, the collectibility of receivables, the classification of liabilities, and the disclosure of contingencies are illustrations. Behind these management assertions are other propositions. The entry of every transaction is itself a proposition based upon analysis of the transaction and leading up to the financial statement amounts and classifications. The deliberate omission of certain transactions from the period's results through cut-off procedures, the selection of inventory prices, the claim to satisfactory internal control procedures—these are also propositions on which judgments must be made by the independent auditor. And many of these subsidiary propositions are interrelated and intermingled, making the recognition and identification of individual propositions very difficult in some cases.

This is not to say that the independent auditor must review every transaction individually. Obviously, he cannot do this. He must, however, satisfy

1

himself as to the general reasonableness of these many subsidiary propositions before he can express an informed opinion on the financial statements as a whole.

Complexity of the opinion

The independent auditor's opinion is complex not only because he has a large number of subsidiary judgments to make, but because the subsidiary propositions to which these judgments relate vary in nature, in significance, and in complexity. Some of them are almost completely quantitative, such as the amount of cash. Others are qualitative—for example, the disclosure or nondisclosure of a contingency. A great many, such as determining the appropriateness of the amount of inventory or receivables, have both quantitative and qualitative aspects. These propositions include both an amount and implications as to usefulness or collectibility, either of which may be crucial in influencing judgments as to the acceptability of the proposition. The variability of these propositions with respect to significance is the ever-present problem of materiality, and it is easy to see that some are much more important than others. Thus it is never just a matter of the number of propositions judged acceptable or unacceptable. Propositions must be evaluated as to materiality as well as acceptability.

We can readily agree, also, that some are more complex than others. The assertion as to the amount of notes payable is generally much simpler than the assertion as to the amount of surplus or of federal income tax payable. These latter rely upon many other propositions, some of which themselves may be of substantial complexity.

Thus, in forming his professional opinion on financial statements, an independent auditor must

somehow deal with a substantial number of widely varying propositions. He must make countless subsidiary judgments; then he must evaluate these, balancing one against another, if necessary; finally he forms an over-all or composite opinion based on all his preliminary judgments.

The problem of judgment formation itself deserves serious consideration. Webster defines the exercise of judgment as "the operation of the mind, involving comparison and discrimination, by which knowledge of values and relations is mentally formulated."[2] Just how the mind operates in making comparisons and discriminations may not be clear, but it seems certain that a well-disciplined mind having available and using pertinent evidential matter will make sounder judgments than an undisciplined mind acting on little more than whim, impulse, or emotion. Another reasonable surmise is that the difficulty of forming an appropriate judgment necessarily will vary with the nature and complexity of the proposition at issue.

The question of certainty

It would seem that our surest judgments occur in areas where we have certain knowledge, but although this is true, it is little comfort. Epistemologists point out that we have very little certain knowledge. When a man says: "I know," he means merely that he is convinced. And how many of us at one time or another have found our firmest convictions in error. Whether it be politics, the anticipated outcome of athletic contests, or expected business results, most of us have had the experience of being absolutely sure — and also dead wrong. Even sensory perceptions are not always reliable. We see a friend in a crowded room, slap him on the shoulder, and find he is a complete stranger. Eyewitnesses to a crime or an accident often differ considerably in their descriptions of what happened. The existence of mirages, look-alikes, and other phenomena, may play havoc with our senses.

In auditing, the problem is at least as difficult as in other fields. Our subject matter is not one that lends itself to easy comprehension. Business facts, their description and measurement, present real difficulties. The more precise measurements of the physical sciences are not available to accountants; neither are their specific designations and descriptions. We have nothing that corresponds to the precision of a chemical formula, for example. Thus the propositions in accounting statements are seldom, if ever, subject to judgment that can be described

R. K. MAUTZ, CPA, Ph.D., is professor of accountancy at the University of Illinois in Urbana. Professor Mautz was a contributing editor of the CPA HANDBOOK, and a former chairman of the Committee on Concepts and Standards of the American Accounting Association. This paper is based on a speech given by Dr. Mautz last fall at the Fifth Annual Tax and Accounting Seminar at the State University of Iowa, and at the 13th Annual Meeting of the North Dakota State Society of CPAs. A previous article by Dr. Mautz on audit evidence appeared in the May 1958 JOURNAL.

[2] Webster's New International Dictionary, Second Edition, Unabridged.

2

appropriately as based on certain knowledge. Only a few purely mathematical facts possess this happy characteristic.

Yet auditing does have the task of proving the propositions in financial statements and must face up to its responsibilities. Here we must be careful of the implications in our terms. To "prove" does not necessarily mean to establish as fact beyond any doubt. If it did, the expression would have little usefulness except in mathematics. Among the accepted meanings of this very useful word are: "1. To try, or to ascertain, by an experiment or by a standard; to test; as, to prove the strength of gunpowder; now, esp., to subject to a technical testing process; as, to prove cannon, gold, coal; also, to try out. . . . 4. To evince, establish, or ascertain by argument, testimony, or other evidence; to demonstrate, show."[3] In auditing, we use the term quite appropriately when we say we *prove* financial statement propositions. That is, we subject them to a technical testing process. Through the application of auditing techniques we gather evidence which we then evaluate to establish the reliability of the propositions at issue. Some we find to be true, some false. But this is no simple task of sorting black from white. The distinctions are not that clear. Among the meanings of "true" is: "Conformable to fact; in accordance with the actual state of things; correct; not false, erroneous, inaccurate, or the like; as a true relation or narration; a true history; a declaration is true when it states the facts."[4]

Acceptance as true or false

If an auditor finds a financial statement proposition to be in accord with business facts as they appear to him at the time of examination, he can accept the proposition as true. If the proposition does not so conform, he must adjudge it false. If the apparent facts are subject to a variety of interpretations, he must seek such evidence as is available to help him in judging the reasonableness of the interpretation advanced by the client. His task is such that judgments must be made, and although he may prefer clear-cut cases of right or wrong, he must judge many propositions that are neither clearly true nor clearly false. Examples might be the desirability of disclosing a given contingency or the appropriate valuation of unlisted investments.

No one would expect a narration or a history to be accurate and complete in every detail, yet if it is substantially faithful to the events it purports to relate, if it is not misleading, then it merits a

description of "true." In the same way, financial statements, in total and in their component propositions, may be "proved" to be "true," that is, they are tested for a reasonable conformity with business events and results. An auditor adopts neither the view of "right unless proved wrong" nor "wrong until proved right." Rather his attitude toward the propositions before him is best described as viewing them as "questionable until tested and found reasonably in accord or at variance with events as he understands them."

Steps in judgment formation

The procedure of judgment formation in auditing must of necessity commence with the individual propositions which in the aggregate make up the financial statements. Only after these have been reviewed and judged is an auditor in position to make his important, over-all judgment. Four closely related but distinct steps are necessary to prove or test any individual proposition. They are:

1. Recognition of the proposition

2. Collection of pertinent evidence

3. Evaluation of the evidence

4. Formation of an opinion as to the conformity of the proposition with events as the auditor understands them

The audit program plays a major role in recognizing individual propositions and providing for the collection of pertinent evidence. Auditors do not follow the practice of making a detailed list of the many propositions before them in an examination and then checking them off one by one as they obtain evidence. They are accustomed to thinking of propositions and dealing with them in groups. To illustrate, the apparently simple assertion "Trade Accounts Payable—$17,000" involves important subsidiary propositions with respect to classification, cut-off, and correlation with inventory and purchases amounts. Some of these may be given individual treatment in the audit program; others may be cared for almost automatically in connection with tests of other propositions. This does not bother an alert, experienced, competent practitioner; it could, of course, prove a real stumbling block to an inexperienced or improperly trained assistant.

The ability to recognize the component propositions in financial statement assertions, to evaluate their significance, and to select appropriate procedures to obtain pertinent evidence on each is not a capacity possessed equally by all. Without a care-

---

[3.] *Webster's New International Dictionary*, Second Edition, Unabridged.

fully planned program to guide him, a novice might well overlook less obvious but none the less significant propositions. Because of the large number of varying propositions included within a set of financial statements, even an experienced auditor may fail to identify and consider them all unless he makes a point of carefully reviewing the adequacy of the audit program in these terms.

Evaluation of audit evidence

The collection and evaluation of evidence proceed, to some extent, simultaneously. As the members of the audit staff perform the various steps in the audit program, they not only collect evidence on which the propriety of financial statement assertions can be judged, they also evaluate that evidence as to pertinence, completeness, and reliability. If they find it inadequate in any of these respects, this fact should be discussed with the engagement supervisor. In addition to this "review as you go," the in-charge auditor normally reviews the evidence gathered by his staff and described in their work papers before initialing them as satisfactory, and the entire file of work papers is then reviewed by the principal.

Like program planning, audit review calls for a high degree of skill, knowledge, and concentration. A competent reviewer exercises analytical ability and judgment of the highest order. At its best, probably no phase of the independent auditor's work is performed with a greater degree of expertness than that of audit review.

In evaluating audit evidence, whether one is a field auditor or a reviewer, he is concerned primarily with the *persuasiveness* of the evidence available. Is it sufficient to persuade him that the given proposition fairly reflects the facts as he understands them? Of course, evidence varies in its influence on the mind of the auditor. The persuasiveness of evidence on a given proposition may be graded roughly somewhat as follows:

1. Absolutely convincing

2. Positively persuasive

3. Neutrally persuasive (i.e., not leading to doubt)

To an experienced auditor, relatively little evidence is convincing. The comfort of complete assurance on any proposition is a rare luxury for at least two reasons, the first of which is the difficulty of attaining sure knowledge. Only on strictly mathematical propositions, such as totals, extensions, and other calculations, can he have complete assurance, and even in these cases his assurance is restricted to the mathematical aspects. He must still have reservations with respect to the components of the calculation until these propositions too have been tested. Secondly, a wise auditor recognizes the danger in permitting himself to be absolutely convinced, for to be convinced is often to close one's mind to alternative possibilities. It is the very essence of auditing that the practitioner keep an open mind and strive to obtain any useful evidence available on both sides of every proposition at issue.

Whereas little audit evidence is convincing, much of it is persuasive. Through the application of auditing techniques, the auditor obtains real, testimonial, or indirect evidence[5] indicating that the company's accounting representations are satisfactorily in accord with actual events and results. Of course, the evidence available may be persuasive in varying degrees. The relative difficulty with which an auditor is persuaded as to the truthfulness of a given proposition is dependent on a variety of factors, one of which is his understanding of the kinds and reliability of audit evidence.

Cases of insufficient evidence

Sometimes, and not infrequently, an auditor finds insufficient evidence to persuade him positively as to a given proposition, but on the other hand a reasonable investigation likewise supplies no reason to doubt the validity of the asserted proposition. Such evidence as is available is neutral; it fails to influence him strongly either for or against the proposition at issue. In such cases he has little alternative to accepting the proposition as true. Its existence as a proposition is something of a prima facie case in its favor. If he has recognized it as a proposition and given some reasonable effort to its consideration, if he finds it not incompatible with propositions on which he has acquired more positive evidence, and if he then has no substantial doubt as to its truthfulness, he is entitled and even bound to accept it as a valid proposition. An auditor has no more right to act by whim or hunch in rejecting financial statement propositions than he has in accepting them. A reasonable investigation that uncovers no reason to doubt the proposition effectively supports it. It has been tested and found not false; in effect, it has been proved "true."

Careful evaluation of the evidence available in most cases leads directly to a conclusion as to the validity of the proposition at issue. Thus judgment

---

[5]See "Reliability of Audit Evidence," JOURNAL OF ACCOUNTANCY, May 1958, for a discussion of the kinds of audit evidence.

4

formation on individual propositions rarely presents an extended problem. Any real difficulty in coming to a judgment implies a lack of sufficient evidence, whether positive or negative, and can generally be remedied by acquiring more. Of course individuals vary; some are more cautious than others. Some are overly hasty, others extremely reluctant. This is one of the reasons why good experience under competent supervision and guidance is important. Through such experience one can season and improve his judgmental ability.

Dangers in judgment formation

Before considering the formulation of the independent auditor's over-all or composite opinion, it may be well to note some of the dangers in audit judgment formation. Apparent as these dangers may be, it is desirable that they be given at least passing attention. The first is the possibility of approval by default, or failing to recognize the existence of a proposition and thereby effectively accepting it. If there is any place where silence may be interpreted as meaning consent, it is in an audit opinion.[6] Failure to raise a question as to the fairness of financial statement presentations must mean that all the propositions in the financial statements, at least all material propositions, are approved as valid. For the statements as a whole to be presented fairly, surely there must be included in them no material propositions that are considered to be at variance with the facts. Thus, if by omission from the audit program we fail to identify a given proposition, to obtain pertinent evidence, and to come to a conclusion as to its validity, we automatically accept it without exposing it to our normal testing procedure. We have defaulted on our responsibility of judgment formation, but we must nevertheless accept responsibility. This is not to say that every proposition in the financial statements must be identified in the audit program. Many of them are not sufficiently material. Others may be judged almost of necessity in connection with other specified propositions. Yet, an experienced auditor will remain alert to the possibility of failure to identify significant propositions, thereby permitting them to pass without submission to the proving process.

Sufficient evidence essential

A second danger may arise from collecting too little evidence. The auditor is obligated to make a "reasonable" investigation and to secure enough evidence to provide sufficient grounds for his decisions.[7] Whether standards indicating desirable kinds and extent of evidence on various propositions can ever be established is questionable, and unless and until such standards can be devised and accepted, individual judgment remains the only guide available.

Relative importance of evidence

Deficient evaluation of evidence, whether resulting from inexperience, carelessness, haste, lack of knowledge, or other cause, is yet another danger. Adequate evaluation, of course, requires an understanding of the nature and relative reliability of the various kinds of evidence and their relation to audit techniques and procedures.

In forming a composite or over-all opinion as to the fairness of presentation of the financial statements, the auditor is concerned not with evidence, but with the relative weight to be accorded his various judgments on the many subsidiary propositions on which he has acquired evidence and formed opinions. At this point he reviews each of these many propositions and his judgment on them, evaluates their importance, balances them against any contrary judgments, and sums them all up. It is like an algebraic summation with both positive and negative elements, some of which are far more important than others. In those cases in which the "untrue" propositions outweigh the "true," the auditor must refrain from giving a standard opinion. If only a few important propositions are unacceptable and a majority are satisfactory, a qualified opinion may be forthcoming. Even a "clean" opinion, however, does not mean that all propositions were proved true; it means only that no material propositions were found to be unsatisfactory. On balance, and taken in the aggregate, they constitute a fair presentation of events and results as the auditor understands them.

Conclusions

Now what is the significance of these remarks? First, that judgment must inevitably play a major role in auditing. Second, that we will do well to recognize this and acquaint ourselves with the process of judgment formation and its application in auditing. Third, that audit evidence is the basis on which opinions rest, and we must understand its usefulness and limitations if we are to meet our responsibilities satisfactorily. Fourth, that auditing, like other fields of professional service, deals not in absolutes but only in relative truths, a fact that is recognized in the phrase "auditor's opinion."

[6]See Rule 5, "Rules of Professional Conduct" of the American Institute of CPAs, as revised January 20, 1958.

[7]See Standard of Field Work No. 3, *Generally Accepted Auditing Standards*, American Institute of CPAs, 1954.

5

A Case Study on the

EXTENT of

AUDIT SAMPLES

Summary audit programs
prepared independently
by 8 different CPAs
to indicate extent of
audit sampling each
considered necessary in
an actual case.

AMERICAN INSTITUTE OF ACCOUNTANTS
The National Professional Society of Certified Public Accountants
270 MADISON AVENUE, NEW YORK 16, N. Y.

CONTENTS

PREFACE

This booklet describes an actual audit situation and presents the views of eight certified public accountants as to the extent of audit sampling each believes would be necessary in the circumstances.

While the results are not conclusive as to what would be the appropriate amount of sampling in a given situation, it is believed that many CPAs will be helped by comparing their views with the views of those who prepared the summary audit programs.

CARMAN G. BLOUGH, *Director of Research*
AMERICAN INSTITUTE OF ACCOUNTANTS

October, 1955

A Case Study on the

EXTENT OF AUDIT SAMPLES

INTRODUCTION

The practicability of using statistical techniques for determining the extent of sampling that would be appropriate in a particular audit engagement has received increasing attention among certified public accountants in recent years. Many accountants have questioned the usefulness of this approach, largely because they hesitate to place reliance on what seem to them to be largely mechanical procedures in an area where judgment and the results of testing as it is actually performed are such important factors. Others have felt that, properly used, statistical techniques can be very helpful.

The committee on auditing procedure of the American Institute of Accountants recently considered the question, but believed that it did not have sufficient information as to the extent of audit sampling in practice to reach any conclusions. Accordingly, as a step in the direction of obtaining more information as to current thinking, a description of an actual business was prepared and distributed to the members of the committee. Each member was asked to submit to the research department his views as to the extent of sampling he thought would be necessary in the particular case in order to express an unqualified opinion. The programs were submitted only to the research department so that no committee member knew what other committee members had suggested.

Although there was some degree of similarity among the views expressed as to the extent of sampling necessary with respect to most

7

11

items on the financial statements, no clear-cut pattern resulted. The committee believes, however, that the information obtained is of considerable interest and value, and that it should be made available to the profession. Accordingly, it asked the research department to publish the description of the business and several of the more complete programs.

A major problem to the authors in the preparation of these programs was the unfamiliarity with the people in the companies and their accounting policies and procedures. As a matter of fact, it is almost impossible for anybody to write a complete story on a client so that the outsider could fully understand it and prepare an audit program based upon the information submitted.

From the auditing standpoint, the preparation of these programs really points up the problem that everyone faces in defining in precise terms exactly what he means when he uses the words "check," "review," or "test." On the other hand, no program is prepared in such a manner that an auditor unfamiliar with the engagement could make an examination solely on the basis of the program.

Another matter that is difficult to spell out in an audit program arises in connection with what to do when errors or differences are disclosed. It is easy enough to say that the auditor should check five per cent of the items and if the results are satisfactory, presumably, no further checking is required. On the other hand, if he does check that five per cent of the items and does find substantial errors or differences then, obviously, he may be required to expand his tests or apply other auditing procedures. To express this fact in words in a specific audit program is exceedingly difficult, and that is the reason why in many places the author is apt to use the word "test," rather than being more specific. Judgment is the most important factor in the making of any audit, but in many situations it is practically impossible to write out in specific language how the auditor applies judgment.

It should be emphasized, therefore, that the programs which follow were prepared entirely from the information contained in the description of the business. Obviously, this precluded any possible judgment by the authors as to such intangibles as the "feel" of the situation and as to additional or reduced work that might be indicated as the audit work progressed. Some of the audit programs summarize general procedures, whereas others emphasize more particularly the descriptions of detailed testing procedures where sampling was considered appropriate. It will also be noted that some of the audit programs contemplate an "initial audit" situation, whereas others are programs applicable on a continuing engagement basis. None of the programs are presented as being "ideal" or as outlining minimum necessary procedures. Other accountants might quite appropriately conduct the examination still differently.

DESCRIPTION OF BUSINESS

Putnam Lumber Company, Inc., was incorporated as a manufacturer of hardwood flooring in 1940. On July 1, 1940, it took over the operations of a partnership doing business as Putnam Lumber Company. The two partners, who were brothers, became the only stockholders of the corporation. At the date of the transfer the net assets of the partnership totaled $251,254.68, of which $200,000.00 was converted to Capital Stock, the balance to Paid-In Surplus.

The management is vested in a board of three directors consisting of the two stockholders and an attorney. One of the brothers is the president, the other is the vice-president and treasurer, and the attorney is the secretary of the company.

The company operates a flooring mill in Johnstown, Tennessee, a small mountain town, and employs approximately fifty men in the mill, two office workers, two warehousemen and two lumber inspectors. The office workers consist of a general ledger bookkeeper and one assistant. The general ledger bookkeeper acts as office manager, keeps all the books with the exception of accounts receivable and inventory (which are kept by the assistant).

The books of account consist of:

A Columnar Journal (in which are entered cash receipts and disbursements, purchases and sales)

13

A General Journal
A General Ledger
Perpetual Inventory Records
Accounts Receivable Ledger
Payroll Records

The company's accounting procedures and its internal control are as follows:

Cash

Practically all the cash received is for payments on accounts receivable and are received by mail. No one person has control over incoming receipts, as they are received at the Post Office by either the two officers or the bookkeepers. The company deposits daily its cash receipts in either the local bank or a bank in a nearby city at which the company has an open line of credit of $500,000. The bank accounts are reconciled by the general ledger bookkeeper and consist of the general bank account and a payroll bank account.

All cash disbursements, with the exception of petty cash items, are made by check, drawn by the general ledger bookkeeper and signed by either of the officer-stockholders. When checks are issued in payment of invoices, the general ledger bookkeeper stamps the invoice "paid" and enters the date and check number thereon and these invoices are presented to the officers at the time of their signing the check. The officers do not always examine the supporting papers to the check but they are available for examination at any time.

Invoices are checked by the general ledger bookkeeper for price, extensions, receipt of goods, etc., before the issuance of checks.

There is a small petty cash fund of $25.00 out of which minor payments are made and which is operated on the imprest basis.

Securities

It is noted from the balance sheet that the company owns a considerable amount of securities. These securities are in a lock box in the city bank which can be entered by either of the two officer-stockholders.

Any notes which the company may have are kept in its safe at the company's office and are in control of the general ledger bookkeeper.

Accounts Receivable

As stated above, the assistant to the bookkeeper maintains accounts receivable. Customers' invoices are prepared by either of the two office workers. The invoices are not pre-numbered. Upon receipt of an order from a customer, which is usually for a carload lot, with an occasional truck load, the lumber is loaded onto the car or truck by the warehousemen who make tallies of the amounts loaded, which tallies are turned into the office. These are extended to obtain the total quantities shipped and the invoice is prepared therefrom.

Monthly statements are mailed to all customers—about fifty in number.

Inventory

Perpetual inventory records are maintained for raw material and finished flooring on hand. These records are kept by the assistant bookkeeper. Purchases of lumber are made exclusively by either of the officer-stockholders. When the lumber is received on the company's yard, quantities are checked by one of the lumber inspectors who turns in lumber tallies to the office, which checks them to the vendor's invoices. If no error exists in the quantities billed by the vendor, checks are immediately issued in payment. No purchase orders are issued.

The company's raw lumber inventory is kept in stacks of approximately 25,000 board feet per stack, and as the lumber is received on the yard the number of board feet in each stack is marked thereon. As the lumber is to be used, it is taken from the stack and loaded on yard truck cars and run through the dry kiln. This process requires from 8 to 10 days. All lumber on hand, even though in the dry kiln, is considered raw material and is not charged into work in process until the cars are pulled from the dry kiln.

Daily production reports of manufactured flooring are made. These reports serve as a basis for the charges to the perpetual inventory.

Fixed Assets

The company does not maintain a plant ledger for fixed assets but does keep a more or less itemized depreciation schedule which shows the larger items in detail and the year of purchase. The smaller items are grouped in the same manner.

The bookkeeper is a very good accountant and consistently capitalizes such items as are proper.

Due to the fact that the company issues a check for lumber purchases immediately upon receipt of the lumber, it never has any accounts payable except for small amounts for mill and other supplies.

Any notes for borrowed money are signed by either of the officer-stockholders.

Payrolls are prepared weekly for mill personnel from clock cards turned in to the office by the mill superintendent. The payrolls are figured by the two office employees and payroll, earnings record, and checks are prepared at one operation. The net amount of the payroll is transferred from the general bank account to the payroll bank account weekly. All payroll checks are signed by one of the officer-stockholders. Checks are usually distributed by one of the officer-stockholders or by the bookkeeper. Salaries of all other employees are paid monthly by checks drawn on the general account.

The company owns 100% of the stock in Putnam Realty Company, which company does logging and sawmill operations and furnishes its entire output of lumber to the Lumber Company at the prevailing market prices on the date of sale.

The accounting records and procedures of the Putnam Realty Company are almost identical to those of the Lumber Company and are kept by the office force of the Lumber Company. Payrolls for the Realty Company are sent in weekly by the superintendent of the logging and sawmill operations on time books which he maintains and the procedure from then on is exactly the same as that of the Lumber Company.

The company desires an opinion report and tax service for both companies but does not want a consolidated report.

FINANCIAL STATEMENTS

Putnam Lumber Company, Inc.

Putnam Realty Company, Inc.

Putnam Lumber Company, Inc. (A Tennessee Corporation)
Johnstown, Tennessee

COMPARATIVE STATEMENT OF OPERATIONS
Years Ended June 30, 1955, and 1954

	Year Ended June 30	
	1955	1954
Sales—Net	$1,339,028.28	3,091,916.42
Cost of Goods Sold		
Inventory—Beginning	260,543.86	529,958.88
Purchases	940,308.02	1,653,384.12
Manufacturing:		
Labor	134,795.70	248,049.32
Superintendence	12,499.96	12,000.00
Supplies	6,183.32	27,805.72
Freight	698.06	2,344.72
Lights and Power	8,567.26	6,082.92
Repairs	17,512.88	80,704.58
Oil	617.80	832.70
Water	544.22	462.26
Depreciation	33,485.88	31,648.62
Repairs and Fuel (Lumber Lift)	3,345.84	5,270.78
Miscellaneous	1,290.44	3,078.74
Seals and Strapping	5,294.50	16,718.36
	1,425,687.74	2,618,341.72
Less—Inventory—Ending	364,072.60	260,543.86
Cost of Goods Sold	1,061,615.14	2,357,797.86
Gross Profit	277,413.14	734,118.56

15

Comparative Statement of Operations (Continued)

	1955	1954
Forward	277,413.14	734,118.56
Selling, General and Administrative Expenses		
Officers' Salaries	44,800.00	48,000.00
Office Salaries	15,000.00	15,200.00
Insurance	9,308.46	8,580.18
Compensation Insurance	3,372.50	4,181.12
Auto Repairs	927.42	280.52
Dues and Subscriptions	4,303.78	8,564.46
Gasoline	1,221.20	1,755.34
Inspection	36,467.80	45,363.52
Postage	250.80	169.16
Supplies	654.18	1,220.90
Payroll Taxes	9,384.96	13,380.78
General Taxes	6,407.58	19,676.98
Legal and Professional	2,583.98	3,411.40
Telephone and Telegraph	2,067.48	2,267.00
Depreciation	2,009.02	2,066.30
Traveling	8,457.94	9,848.02
Exchange	—	33.50
Miscellaneous	1,095.50	2,257.28
TOTAL SELLING, GENERAL AND ADMINISTRATIVE EXPENSES	148,312.60	186,256.46
Net Operating Profit	$129,100.54	547,862.10
Other Income		
Discounts Earned	15,008.08	29,178.78
Rents	432.80	583.14
Dividends Received	18,427.04	13,649.94
Sales Tax Compensation	21.30	37.90
Gain on Sale of Fixed Assets	800.92	1,000.00
Interest	250.00	263.34
Coca Cola Machine	670.40	—
TOTAL OTHER INCOME	35,610.54	44,713.10
	164,711.08	592,575.20

16

Comparative Statement of Operations (Continued)

	1955	1954
Forward	164,711.08	592,575.20
Other Deductions		
Discounts Allowed	26,307.18	59,584.80
Life Insurance (Net)	—	416.68
Bad Debts	39,672.66	740.00
Depreciation—Rental Property	679.02	679.02
Donations	2.290.00	550.00
TOTAL OTHER DEDUCTIONS	68,948.86	61,970.50
Profit before Federal Income Tax	95,762.22	530,604.70
Provision for Federal Income Tax	44,296.35	241,868.88
Net Profit for Year	$ 51,465.87	288,735.82

STATEMENT OF SURPLUS
Years Ended June 30, 1955, and 1954

	1955	1954
Balance, Beginning of Period	$1,530,216.30	1,241,480.48
Net Profit for Year	51,465.87	288,735.82
	1,581,682.17	1,530,216.30
LESS—1952-53 Additional Income Taxes	6,477.44	—
Surplus, End of Period	$1,575,204.73	1,530,216.30

17

ASSETS	1955	1954
Current Assets		
Cash	$ 509,471.54	692,061.86
Temporary Investment—Stocks	408,448.00	408,448.00
Accounts Receivable—Customers	85,151.88	161,273.84
Accounts Receivable—Employees	156.18	1,827.96
Accounts Receivable—Other	—	59,972.56
Notes Receivable	10,000.00	10,000.00
Interest Receivable	513.34	263.34
Inventories (At Lower of Cost or Market)	364,072.60	260,543.86
TOTAL CURRENT ASSETS	1,377,813.54	1,594,391.42
Other Assets		
Accounts Receivable—Officers	25,398.74	29,498.74
Accounts Receivable—Putnam Realty Company	52,759.58	—
Investments—Putnam Realty Company	35,405.40	35,405.40
Real Estate (Not Used in Business)	83,037.98	83,037.98
Deposits	1,800.00	1,800.00
Coca Cola Box	—	240.40
TOTAL OTHER ASSETS	198,401.70	149,982.52
Fixed Assets (at cost)		
Land	8,027.20	8,027.20
Buildings	212,471.60	212,471.60
Automobiles and Trucks	34,396.12	37,468.86
Machinery and Equipment	245,209.84	245,209.84
Sprinkler System	6,269.44	6,269.44
Spur Track	1,747.02	1,747.02
Yard Tracks	20,422.30	20,422.30
Office Equipment	8,086.22	7,476.22
Binkley House	13,580.20	13,580.20
TOTAL	550,209.94	552,672.68
LESS—Reserve for Depreciation	244,317.12	213,516.86
NET VALUE FIXED ASSETS	305,892.82	339,155.82
Deferred Charges		
Prepaid Taxes and Licences	354.78	55.50
Unexpired Insurance	4,681.46	5,106.12
TOTAL DEFERRED CHARGES	5,036.24	5,161.62
	$1,887,144.30	2,088,691.38

18

LIABILITIES AND CAPITAL	1955	1954
Current Liabilities		
Accounts Payable	$ 8,380.60	6,116.93
Accrued Taxes	8,007.94	12,786.55
Provision for Federal Income Tax	44,296.35	241,868.88
TOTAL CURRENT LIABILITIES	60,684.89	260,772.36

Other Liabilities

Accounts Payable—Officers	—	46,448.04

Capital

Capital Stock		
Common	200,000.00	200,000.00
Surplus—Paid In	51,254.68	51,254.68
Surplus—Earned	1,575,204.73	1,530,216.30
TOTAL CAPITAL	1,826,459.41	1,781,470.98
	$1,887,144.30	2,088,691.38

19

23

Putnam Realty Company (A Tennessee Corporation)
Johnstown, Tennessee

COMPARATIVE STATEMENT OF OPERATIONS
Years Ended June 30, 1955, and 1954

| | Year Ended June 30 | |
	1955	1954
Sales	$192,072.24	149,374.14
Cost of Sales		
Inventory, Beginning of Period	50,814.66	4,843.40
Depletion of Standing Timber	37,160.68	25,285.30
Saw Mill Expenses:		
Supervision	8,200.00	9,200.00
Labor	93,803.34	71,528.64
Freight	—	311.56
Automobile and Truck Expense	12,443.04	12,710.24
Travel Expense	374.00	94.08
Repairs	5,786.34	7,784.14
Depreciation	11,161.38	10,362.18
Sundry	239.40	27.78
	219,982.84	142,147.32
LESS—Inventory, End of Period	16,749.22	50,814.66
COST OF SALES	203,233.62	91,332.66
Gross Profit (Loss)	(11,161.38)	58,041.48

20

24

Comparative Statement of Operations (Continued)

	1955	1954
Forward	(11,161.38)	58,041.48
General and Administrative Expenses		
Officers' Salaries	5,000.00	10,000.00
State Bond	300.00	300.00
Taxes	6,835.64	6,696.36
Insurance	1,151.68	490.98
Legal and Professional	530.16	827.32
Office Supplies	—	75.44
Repairs	7.84	117.06
Traveling	—	113.00
Sundry	721.10	8,698.70
TOTAL GENERAL AND ADMINISTRATIVE EXPENSES	14,546.42	27,318.86
	(25,707.80)	30,722.62
Other Income		
Interest	357.92	281.98
Discounts Taken	11.18	40.86
Rent	8,000.00	7,842.58
Gain on Sale of Fixed Assets	—	6,845.96
TOTAL OTHER INCOME	8,369.10	15,011.38
	(17,338.70)	45,734.00
Other Deductions		
Discounts Allowed	291.36	7.42
Farm Expense	13,300.12	—
Interest	1,678.74	2,967.98
TOTAL OTHER DEDUCTIONS	15,270.22	2,975.40
Profit Before Federal Taxes	(32,608.92)	42,758.60
Provision for Federal Income Taxes	—	16,369.80
Net Profit for Year	(32,608.92)	26,388.80

21

25

ASSETS	1955	1954
Current Assets		
Cash	$ 16,027.02	31,186.96
Notes Receivable	14,270.00	10,270.00
Accrued Interest Receivable	489.90	251.98
Inventory—Lumber (At Cost)	16,749.22	50,814.66
TOTAL CURRENT ASSETS	47,536.14	92,523.60
Other Assets		
Deposits	20.00	173.96
Farm (Not Used in Business)	21,013.78	—
TOTAL OTHER ASSETS	21,033.78	173.96
Fixed Assets		
Land	59,065.42	57,565.42
Buildings	—	4,125.50
Automobiles and Trucks	5,099.50	4,615.00
Logging Equipment	54,663.40	54,663.40
Machinery and Equipment	35,524.96	27,016.14
	154,353.28	147,985.46
LESS—Reserve for Depreciation	49,575.18	39,561.30
	104,778.10	108,424.16
Timber Rights (Less Depletion)	23,386.48	60,547.16
TOTAL FIXED ASSETS	128,164.58	168,971.32
Deferred Charges		
Prepaid Taxes	68.36	87.24
Unexpired Insurance	254.72	330.52
TOTAL DEFERRED CHARGES	323.08	417.76
	$197,057.58	262,086.64

LIABILITIES AND CAPITAL	1955	1954
Current Liabilities		
Notes Payable	$ 6,250.00	42,500.00
Accrued Payroll	2,585.70	12,208.50
Accrued Interest	330.14	1,296.24
Accrued Taxes	2,257.66	2,490.56
Provision for Federal Taxes	—	16,369.80
TOTAL CURRENT LIABILITIES	11,423.50	74,865.10
Other Liabilities		
Accounts Payable—Putnam Lumber		
Company	52,759.58	—
Notes Payable	—	21,250.00
TOTAL OTHER LIABILITIES	52,759.58	21,250.00
Deferred Income		
Rent Collected in Advance	4,000.00	4,000.00
Interest Collected in Advance	270.00	270.00
TOTAL DEFERRED INCOME	4,270.00	4,270.00
Capital		
Capital Stock—Common—		
Issued and Outstanding	29,800.00	29,800.00
Surplus—Arising from Revaluation		
of Standing Timber	16,898.58	16,898.58
Earned Surplus	81,905.92	115,002.96
TOTAL CAPITAL	128,604.50	161,701.54
	$197,057.58	262,086.64

23

SUMMARY AUDIT PROGRAMS

ACCOUNTANT "A"

The development of conclusions with respect to the appropriate extent of the audit sample is complicated by the fact that the extent of the sample depends upon the degree of reliance which the auditor can place on the effectiveness of the client company's system of internal accounting control, which effectiveness itself can only be measured by means of sampling techniques. Therefore, it appears that the development of criteria with respect to the adequacy of audit samples must be considered from the point of view of the extent of sampling required to (1) appraise the effectiveness of the company's internal accounting control and (2) form an opinion with respect to the individual accounts being maintained under specific conditions of internal accounting control.

Effectiveness of Internal Control

Because the effectiveness of a company's system of internal accounting control does not remain constant, due to changes in personnel, fluctuations in volume of business, etc., the auditor cannot rely completely upon his knowledge from previous examinations, although the extent of his tests in this respect can be limited to some degree on the basis of his former experience with the company. In the case study, if this were the first examination of the accounts of the companies, a minimum test of at least three months' detail cash transactions would be required. However, assuming the auditor has performed previous examinations and has determined that he can place a considerable degree of reliance on the system of internal accounting control, a minimum test of one month's transactions might be satisfactory, with an extension of the tests if the controls do not appear to be operating as effectively as in prior years.

The extent of the sampling required to ascertain the effectiveness of existing controls depends upon the reliance which the auditor places on the adequacy of the controls themselves from his previous familiarity with the company's procedures. For instance, if established controls over cash receipts and accounts receivable are weak, as in the case study, the auditor may desire to test as many as 15 days' authenticated deposit slips to the cash and receivables records to ascertain that the existing minimum aspects of control are operating effectively. If the bookkeeper has been found previously to be completely familiar with the proper accounting treatment to be accorded capital and expense items, the extent of the test of property additions and repair expense items may be limited to a few major items as a test of the effectiveness of existing controls.

Statement and Classification of Individual Accounts

Regardless of the degree of effectiveness of the company's system of internal accounting control, certain minimum audit procedures which utilize sampling techniques must be applied to determine that particular accounts are stated properly. For instance, cash balances require confirmation, a number of accounts receivable require circularization, a portion of inventories must be observed and price-tested, certain additions and retirements to the property accounts must be investigated to determine the propriety of accounting treatment accorded these items, and so on.

The extent of the test of specific accounts is not only dependent upon the degree of internal accounting control with respect to the particular account, but also upon the importance of the account relative to other accounts. For instance, as in the case study, property accounting controls may be satisfactory and operating effectively, but the account is of such importance to the statements as a whole that the extent of the examination of transactions in the account may exceed the extent of the examination of the support for transactions in the unexpired insurance account, where controls may be weak, but which is insignificant in amount compared to the property account.

Method of Sampling

Whether the test-checking is used to ascertain the effectiveness of existing internal accounting controls or to form an opinion regarding the proper statement and classification of an individual account, the accountant uses judgment to determine whether to select (1) a random sample (individual items selected at random), (2) a spot sample (a series of items from a specific sequence or period), or (3) specific items as to nature or amount. For instance, in testing to detect the possibility of lapping, the auditor would probably select a spot sample or several spot samples of deposit slips to be authenticated and agreed to the records as the most effective method of determining whether there is evidence of fraud. However, to ascertain that major repair expenses are properly noncapital items, he may desire to select a sample of material items. The type of sample and the number of items selected are based upon the auditor's judgment, and depend upon (1) the purpose of the test and (2) the composition of the account with respect to the volume of transactions, the amount of individual transactions, and the total amount involved as compared to other accounts.

AUDIT PROGRAM

PUTNAM LUMBER COMPANY, INC.
PUTNAM REALTY COMPANY, INC.

AUDIT PROCEDURE	EXTENT OF SAMPLING NECESSARY	COMMENTS
General		
1. Review the minutes of the meetings of the board of directors.	Minutes of all meetings.	To discover management decisions pertaining to accounting matters.
2. Submit a memorandum to the company on the deficiencies of internal accounting control.		
Cash		
1. Count petty cash fund and any cash on hand.	100% of cash on hand.	To see whether there is evidence of possible irregularities in the handling of cash.
(a) Reconcile undeposited receipts with entries in cash receipts journal and deposits.		
2. Select an interim month, and comprehensively examine cash transactions for the period.	All transactions for the one month selected at random, with minor exceptions noted	To determine that cash balances as stated are actually on deposit. To ascertain

below. If the cash records or supporting papers are maintained inadequately, and it is discovered that invoices are not being checked properly for prices, extensions, receipt of goods, etc., the test should be extended to include the transactions of several months.

that internal control surrounding the handling of cash transactions is adequate to provide reasonable assurance against the perpetration and concealment of irregularities.

(a) Obtain beginning and ending reconciliation prepared by the bookkeeper.
  (1) Trace bank balances to bank statements.
  (2) Foot outstanding checks.
  (3) Check other reconciling items.
  (4) Trace book balances to general ledger.

(b) Test disbursements.
  (1) Compare all checks which cleared through the bank during the month with cash journal for the month or the list of outstanding checks at the end of the prior month.

35

Audit Procedure	Extent of Sampling Necessary	Comments

Cash (Cont'd)

(2) Run tape of checks and reconcile to disbursements per bank statement, as computed by reference to the beginning and ending balance on the bank statement and deposits.

(3) Examine check perforations.

(4) Test endorsements on checks.

(5) Foot and crosscast all columns of the cash disbursements and purchases journals.

(6) Check all postings from the cash disbursements and purchases journals to the general ledger.

(c) Test receipts.

(1) Check deposits from cash receipts journal to bank statement.

(2) Foot and crosscast all columns of the cash receipts journal.

(3) Check all postings from cash receipts journal to general ledger.

36

(4) Recompute cash discounts taken for 5% of transactions, and review monthly discounts in relation to monthly cash collections.

(5) Have 15 consecutive days' deposit slips authenticated by the bank. Trace the individual items shown on deposit slips to the cash receipts journal and to customers ledger cards.

(d) Account for transfers to the payroll account and other interbank and intercompany transfers.

(e) Follow-up.

(1) Obtain bank statement and paid checks which cleared through the bank for the period of at least 10 days following the ending reconciliation date.

(2) Trace checks dated prior to the reconciliation date to the cash disbursements journal and to the list of outstanding checks.

(3) Trace large checks dated subsequent to the reconciliation date to the cash disbursements journal, inspecting first bank stamp to determine that checks were not actually issued

Cash (Cont'd)

AUDIT PROCEDURE

prior to the reconciliation date.

(4) Observe that there is no delay in clearing checks drawn at or near the end of the period to ascertain that the cash disbursements journal was not held open.

(f) General.

(1) Confirm bank balances as of the date of the ending reconciliation.

(2) Inspect invoices, purchased lumber tallies, and other underlying documents supporting selected cash disbursements as to:

EXTENT OF SAMPLING NECESSARY

Selected cash disbursements should include a variety of transactions affecting all accounts normally used during the month. The amount of the individual items tested is not significant. It is assumed that the examination of invoices will include approximately 90% of the

COMMENTS

Because of the limited number of the company's personnel, normal aspects of internal accounting control are not practicable. This test should provide a reasonable basis for disclosing possible significant irregularities.

company's normal monthly transactions.

a. Reasonableness of accounting distribution.
b. Evidence of receipt of goods or services.
c. Approval of price and terms.
d. Check of arithmetical accuracy.
e. Agreement of name of vendor per invoice with payee per check.
f. Ascertain that cash discounts were taken when allowed.
g. Test purchase prices to trade journals and other published market quotations.

(3) Examine the data supporting several petty cash reimbursements for authenticity, propriety, and reasonableness.

3. Select one payroll period for the weekly mill payroll and monthly salary payroll and:

(a) Prove arithmetical accuracy of payroll sheets.
(b) Trace payroll account distributions through to the general ledger.

AUDIT PROCEDURE	EXTENT OF SAMPLING NECESSARY	COMMENTS
Cash (Cont'd)		
(c) Test payroll data in detail for 15 employees (including 1 office worker, 1 warehouseman, and 1 inspector).	30% of all company personnel for one pay period.	A random sample of this sort should disclose any weaknesses in the computation of the various types of payroll.
(1) Trace hours to the time cards of mill employees or to the time books of logging and saw mill department personnel.		
(2) Check rates of pay with personnel record cards, labor union contract, or directly with one of the officers.		
(3) Examine authorizations for deductions.		
(4) Check calculations of earnings and deductions.		
(5) Trace earnings to individual record of earnings.		
(6) Trace net earnings from payroll journal to paid checks, and compare endorsements to W-4 statements.		
(7) Observe and control a pay-off.		
(d) Reconcile the payroll bank account for one interim month. (Follow procedures in step 2 above, where applicable.)	The comparison of payroll checks to the payroll journal should be limited to ap-	All transactions are of a similar nature.

proximately 20% of payroll checks. The test of endorsement should be made with reference to employees' W-4 statements signed by employees and should be limited to 10% of employees.

4. Proof of year-end balances.

   (a) Obtain copies of year-end reconciliations prepared by the company, and prove clerical accuracy thereof.

   (b) Confirm bank balances.

   (c) Check reconciliation balances with bank statement, cashbook, and general ledger.

   (d) Obtain directly from the bank statements and paid checks which cleared through the bank for at least the first 10 days following the year end.

   (e) Trace checks dated on or before the year end to the cash disbursements book and list of outstanding checks.

   (f) Determine whether the cashbook appears to have been held open.

   (g) Examine invoices in support of larger checks still outstanding.

Audit Procedure	Extent of Sampling Necessary	Comments
Cash (Cont'd)		
(h) Ascertain that intercompany and interbank transfers for at least a week before and after the year end were recorded in the proper period.		
(i) Review cash transactions up to and subsequent to the balance sheet date, and investigate unusual or material transactions.		
Temporary Investments		
1. Count securities and relate income therefrom to the applicable income accounts.	100%	To account for physical evidence of ownership.
2. Determine the market value of securities at the year end, and agree dividend income to published dividend records.	100%	To ascertain that the basis of valuation of investments is in accordance with generally accepted principles.
3. Account for all changes during year by reference to brokers' advices, etc.	100%	
Accounts Receivable—Customers		
1. Obtain a copy of the trial balance of accounts receivable.		

42

2. Foot and agree total to general ledger.

3. Trace balances of all accounts from the trial balance to the detail ledger.

4. Confirm by positive circularization requests, with open item statements attached, at least 15 customers accounts (30%), to include at least 60% of the total amount of the accounts receivable outstanding. Select specifically the larger account balances outstanding and certain of the smaller accounts at random.

Although the composition of accounts receivable is not known, circularization of at least 30% of the total number of accounts and 60% of the total dollar value of accounts receivable would be necessary.

Because of the small number of total accounts, it would be feasible to circularize 100% of accounts receivable. However, the minimum sample selected would be adequate to determine that the accounts are bona fide. Total accounts receivable represent only 6% of current total assets.

5. Analyze the accounts receivable control account in the general ledger for one month, reconciling charges and credits to contra accounts.
(a) Examine at least 20% of the sales invoices issued during the month.

20% of invoices for one month.

Company's invoicing procedures are weak and there apparently is no internal check of billings.

43

AUDIT PROCEDURE	EXTENT OF SAMPLING NECESSARY	COMMENTS
Accounts Receivable—Customers (Cont'd) (1) Test pricing and arithmetical accuracy. (2) Trace charges to accounts receivable as to date and amount. (3) Examine loading tallies in support of shipments, and test arithmetical accuracy of tallies. (b) Foot sales journal for the month selected for detail review. Trace totals of all columns to general ledger. (c) If practicable, relate feet of lumber and flooring sold to relief of the perpetual inventory record.	If this step can be performed only by tracing individual shipments from the perpetual inventory record to sales invoices, the step should, nevertheless, be performed for 100% of one month's shipments.	The large sample is necessary to ascertain that all shipments are being billed because the company does not control shipping tallies or sales invoices by numerical sequence.
6. Secure from the company an age analysis of accounts receivable. (a) Test at least 10 accounts (20%) for the accuracy of the		

aging and determine the adequacy of the company's estimate of uncollectible accounts receivable, if any.

(b) Review ledger record and correspondence relating to collection efforts with respect to accounts receivable charged off. Ascertain that the officers have approved charge-offs of bad debts. Confirm larger unusual charge-offs.

Investigate all accounts charged off.	To reveal possible evidence of fictitious write-off of bad debts.

7. Test the company's sales cutoff by selecting the sales invoices for a five-day period immediately preceding and subsequent to the year end.

If this test is performed at an interim date for reliance upon the company's control of sales cutoff at the year end, a random sample of invoices, without regard to the amount of the individual transaction, should be selected for test. If the test is performed at the year end, all larger and selected smaller transactions should be investigated in order to ascertain that a significant amount of in-	To ascertain that revenues and costs charged against revenues are accounted for in the proper period.

AUDIT PROCEDURE	EXTENT OF SAMPLING NECESSARY	COMMENTS
Accounts Receivable—Customers (Cont'd)	come was recorded in the proper period.	
(a) Agree the dates that the sales were recorded and the quantities sold with bills of lading and loading tallies.		
(b) Trace posting of invoices tested to accounts receivable ledger cards as to date and amount.		
(c) Trace shipments to relief of perpetual inventory records.		
8. Obtain representations from the officers with respect to the authenticity of accounts and notes receivable.		
Accounts Receivable—Employees		
1. Review the transactions in the general ledger for the year and investigate large or unusual items.		The insignificance of this asset compared to the other assets makes confirmation unnecessary.
2. Agree the total of the detail ledger with the general ledger control at the year end.		

46

Notes Receivable and Interest Receivable

1. Inspect notes receivable and review credit reports for applicable customers.	100%	To determine reasonableness of amount provided for uncollectible accounts.
2. Confirm notes receivable.	100%	To determine notes are bona fide.
3. Analyze note transactions in the general ledger and trace proceeds to the cash receipts book.	All larger transactions and selected others throughout the year.	To reveal possible evidence of irregularity with respect to collection of notes.
4. Relate interest earned to the income, deferred income, and accrued interest receivable accounts.		To determine that income is recorded in the proper period.

Inventories

1. Review the company's cost accounting procedures and its method of maintaining perpetual inventory records and of determining the cost of lumber, work-in-process, and finished flooring inventories. (See also statement of operations, step 1.)	Select one month at random.	To determine the degree of reliance that can be placed upon the company's cost accounting procedures for providing adequate data for the valuation of inventories.
(a) Analyze each inventory control account for one month. tracing major transactions to the original source docu-		

47

AUDIT PROCEDURE	EXTENT OF SAMPLING NECESSARY	COMMENTS
Inventories (Cont'd) ments, such as daily production reports. Test the post-ing of transfers of materials to perpetual inventory de-tail records to the extent necessary to determine that the procedures are adequate and are being executed properly. (b) If practicable, compare the quantity of lumber relieved from raw material inventory with the quantity of floor-ing produced, and determine that the yield loss appears to be reasonable.		
2. Observe the taking of physical inventories of flooring and lumber. Test count and record a number of stacks of lum-ber and finished flooring, the extent of the test to depend up-on the familiarity and ability of employees with the taking of the inventory. (a) If it is not practicable to observe the lumber in the dry kiln, examine the company's book records with respect	Observe the counting of at least 75% of the total value of inventory and test count from 5% to 20% of the total quantity.	To determine that the com-pany has taken reasonable care in the determination of physical quantities. To as-certain that amounts shown as inventories are represent-ed by physical goods.

48

to these items and ascertain that the quantity recorded as in the kiln at the year end appears to be reasonable.

3. Trace the recorded test counts to the adjusted perpetual inventory records and to the company's final inventory summary, and investigate significant overages or shortages.

4. Test the valuation of inventories.

(a) Agree raw material prices to invoices.

Larger quantities of more costly items and selected other items from various sections of the inventory.

To ascertain that prices are fairly determined in accordance with accepted accounting principles, and to detect significant errors in valuation.

(b) Agree unit prices of work-in-process and finished goods inventory to the cost records. (See also step 1 above.)

Ditto.

(c) Ascertain that current replacement cost of inventories is equal to or in excess of the company's costs.

(d) Ascertain that current selling prices exceed finished goods values.

Ditto.

5. Test the clerical accuracy of the compilation of the physical inventory and agree total to the general ledger.

Scan footings and extensions on all pages of the inventory compilation.

A rough test of calculations will disclose any significant arithmetical errors.

Audit Procedure	Extent of Sampling Necessary	Comments
Inventories (Cont'd)		
6. Test the purchases cutoff as of the physical inventory date, by reference to larger vendors invoices and receiving records during the five-day period immediately preceding and subsequent to the year end.	Larger purchases.	To determine that there are no material misstatements of inventory and income as a result of an inadequate cutoff.
(a) Trace purchases of raw materials to the perpetual inventory records to ascertain that the material was taken into account during the proper period.		
7. Secure written representation from officers with respect to inventory principles and procedures.		
Accounts Receivable—Officers		
1. Analyze the control account and the general ledger in detail for a period of at least one month, examining supporting sales invoices, receipts for advances, etc., and trace cash receipts to cash receipts record. Investigate large or unusual transactions in the remaining months.	All transactions for one month and large or unusual transactions in other months.	To determine the nature of officer - company transactions and to detect possible unusual or irregular transactions in view of the close financial relationship of the officers to the company.

2. Confirm the balances with officers at the year end.

100%

To ascertain that the accounts are bona fide.

Accounts Receivable—Putnam Realty Company, Inc.

1. Analyze the control account and the general ledger in detail for a period of at least one month. Investigate large or unusual transactions in the remaining months.

All transactions for one month and large or unusual transactions in other months.

To determine usual nature of transactions and to detect possible unusual or irregular transactions in view of close relationship between the companies.

Investments—Putnam Realty Company, Inc.

1. Examine stock of Putnam Realty Company, Inc.

2. Compare the book value of Putnam Realty Company, Inc., with the investment cost shown on the lumber company's books.

Real Estate (Not Used in Business)
Farm (Not Used in Business)

1. If this is the first examination, inspect recorded deeds and title policies and visit the property. Follow this procedure with respect to larger additions to real estate.

Audit Procedure	Extent of Sampling Necessary	Comments
Real Estate and Farm Not Used in Business (Cont'd)		
2. Inquire into the reasons for the acquisition of the farm and examine invoices supporting the purchase.		
3. Compare description of property on tax receipts, insurance policies, etc., with book records.		
Deposits		
1. Confirm recorded deposits.	All deposits in excess of $50.	Although the item is insignificant when compared to total assets, confirmation is recommended because deposits are susceptible to misappropriation.
Coca Cola Box		
1. Review account in the general ledger, investigating any unusual transactions.	Investigate unusual transactions only.	Funds are susceptible to fraud but the account is not significant compared to related accounts.
Fixed Assets		
1. Review transactions in the general ledger, examining in-	Check larger items only.	To determine that property

52

accounts are stated properly. Since there are few transactions in the accounts, only significant items need be examined in detail.

voices and other data supporting larger purchases during the year. (See real estate program for audit procedure with respect to land acquisitions.)

2. Trace larger additions to the itemized depreciation and depletion schedules.

3. Ascertain that the accounting treatment accorded retirements or sales of property is proper and trace proceeds of sales of real estate, property, timber rights, etc., to the cash receipts journal.

4. Test the arithmetical computations of the itemized depreciation schedule and agree depreciation for the year to the income accounts. Test the computation of depletion and agree amount to income account.

5. Relate gain or loss on sale of fixed assets to income account.

Deferred Charges

1. Examine major insurance policies and agree details to company's record of total premiums in the process of amortization.

53

Audit Procedure	Extent of Sampling Necessary	Comments
Deferred Charges (Cont'd)		
(a) Examine larger invoices supporting insurance expenditures.		
(b) Roughly test mathematical computation of periodic charges to income and details of major unexpired premiums.		
(c) Roughly test compensation insurance expense based upon actual payrolls.		
(d) Ascertain that coverage is adequate for usual risks.		
2. Generally review for reasonableness the company's schedule setting forth details of prepaid taxes and licenses. (See also program with respect to accrued liabilities.)	General review unless unusual items observed.	Minor items, such as licenses, can be accepted on the basis of a general review.
Notes Payable		
1. Confirm the amount, terms, and collateral to all significant recorded notes payable.	All significant notes.	Confirmation is the only satisfactory proof of the nature and extent of the company's liability.

2. Analyze and compare the interest account with the recorded note transactions to ascertain that there are no unrecorded notes on which interest has been paid.

3. Examine canceled paid notes in support of recorded loan payments as evidence of discharge of obligations.

Accounts Payable

1. Foot and agree detail record of accounts payable with the general ledger control account. Examine invoices and receiving records in support of larger items.

2. Make a search for unrecorded liabilities by examining invoices and receiving records supporting July purchases and disbursements.

   Examine invoices over $300.

   Confirmation of accounts payable would appear to be unnecessary. The search for unrecorded liabilities should disclose any unrecorded items, and the examination of checks in support of subsequent payments should disclose the authenticity of recorded items.

3. Examine file of unentered invoices.

Audit Procedure	Extent of Sampling Necessary	Comments
Accounts Payable (Cont'd)		
4. Examine checks in payment of accounts payable at the year end.		
5. Obtain written representation from the officers to the effect that all liabilities have been recorded at the balance-sheet date.		
Accrued Liabilities and Provision for Federal Income Taxes		
1. Analyze accrued tax and accrued interest accounts for the entire year, agreeing total accruals to the relative charges to income.		To ascertain that taxes are being computed properly and that the liability at the year end is accurate.
(a) Examine tax bills, returns, and receipts in support of 50% of payments of each type of tax.		
(b) Review computation of taxes by reference to payrolls, sales, etc., and test arithmetical accuracy for at least one payment of each type of tax.		
(c) Review returns supporting year-end tax accruals and examine canceled checks in payment thereof.		

2. Agree accrued payroll to payroll totals including proration of split period.

Other Liabilities

1. See program for (1) accounts receivable—Putnam Realty Company, Inc., (2) notes payable, and (3) accounts receivable—officers.

Deferred Income

1. Examine leases. Scan the control accounts in the general ledger and agree clearings to rental income account. Trace rents received for several months to the cash receipts book. (See also notes receivable and interest receivable, step 4.)

General review for reasonableness.

To determine that accounting treatment is in accordance with lease agreement.

Capital Stock and Surplus

1. Analyze changes in capital and surplus accounts and agree net profit or loss for the year and other items to related accounts.

2. Agree the total shares of capital stock shown as outstanding by the stock ledger with the shares indicated as outstanding by the general ledger account and examine the stock certificate book to account for all unissued certificates.

3. Consider the propriety of the company's treatment of surplus

57

Audit Procedure	Extent of Sampling Necessary	Comments
Capital Stock and Surplus (Cont'd) arising from the revaluation of timber in the light of chapter 9(b) of A.I.A. Accounting Research Bulletin No. 43.		
Statement of Operations		
1. Examine company's monthly operating statements for an over-all analysis of sales and revenues and costs and expenses.	Review for unusual transactions and business trends.	A general review will disclose possible losses for which provision should be made, cost trends which may affect inventory valuation, etc.
2. Compare income accounts with prior year and inquire into unusual changes, i.e., repairs, supplies, seals and strapping, dues and subscriptions, general taxes, etc.		
3. Scan the accounts in the general ledger for reasonableness and ascertain the reason for monthly fluctuations. Investigate the nature of charges to unfamiliar accounts, i.e., repairs and fuel (lumber lift), seals and strappings, dues and subscriptions, farm expense, etc.	The auditor should be familiar with the nature of charges to all accounts on the company's books.	It should not be necessary to examine charges to minor accounts, such as freight, oil, water, automobile repairs, postage, etc., if

4. Select the following accounts for the examination of invoices of larger amounts.

the auditor is familiar with the nature of the expenditures from previous examinations.

Examine repair items in excess of $300, legal and professional expense items over $100, and all donations.

Since the reason for the test is to bring to our attention unusual items, the examination of a block of invoices or other random sample would not determine whether the proper accounting treatment was accorded to major items.

(a) Repairs and repairs and fuel (lumber lift): To detect items which are properly chargeable to capital accounts.

(b) Legal and other professional: To determine possible liability of the company in connection with lawsuits.

(c) Donations: To determine whether donations are deductible for federal income tax purposes.

5. Select the following accounts for the examination of a selection of invoices: Manufacturing supplies, purchases, inspec-

The extent of the sample depends upon the composi-

The principal purpose of the review of these accounts

AUDIT PROCEDURE

Statement of Operations (Cont'd)

tion, travel, automobile expense, and farm expense.

EXTENT OF SAMPLING
NECESSARY

tion of the accounts with respect to (1) volume of
transactions, (2) amounts
of individual and monthly
transactions, and (3) number of vendors involved. If
there are a large number of
charges, similar in amount
from various vendors, and
the total amount is approximately the same monthly,
select for test a block of invoices at random from one
month's business. If there
are a large number of charges with extreme variations
in amount from various vendors, and the total amount
varies monthly, select for

COMMENTS

is to determine the effectiveness of the established controls over payment and accounting distribution.

test the larger invoices and selected smaller ones from several months' business containing the greater amount of charges.

All invoices affecting two months' business.

It is assumed that the monthly charges to these accounts will be few in number and in approximately equal amounts from one or a few vendors. A sample such as this will be sufficient to indicate whether accounting controls are operating effectively.

6. Select the following accounts for the examination of invoices affecting several months' business: Light and power and telephone and telegraph.

7. The following accounts are tested in connection with the review of related balance-sheet accounts:

Income account	*Related balance-sheet account*
Sales	Accounts receivable
Labor	Cash

Audit Procedure	Extent of Sampling Necessary	Comments
Statement of Operations (Cont'd)		
Supervision — Cash		
Depreciation — Fixed assets		
Officers' salaries — Cash		
Office salaries — Cash		
Insurance — Deferred charges		
Compensation insurance — Deferred charges		
Payroll taxes — Accrued liabilities		
General taxes — Accrued liabilities		
Discounts earned — Cash		
Dividends received — Investments		
Gain on sale of fixed assets — Fixed assets		
Interest — Notes receivable and interest receivable		
Bad debts — Accounts receivable		
Provision for federal income tax — Accrued liabilities.		

It is believed that a program cannot indicate rigidly in advance the extent of sampling to be used in verification of accounts. A review of internal control procedures and the results of tests as they progress will indicate what portion of the detail the test should encompass, but any indicated percentage of sampling must be considered flexible until the auditor has satisfied himself as to the accuracy of the account involved. It is doubtful that any valid generalizations can be drawn as to the extent of such sampling. The following is presented as a tentative program of extent of sampling of the principal accounts subject to adjustment during the actual examination on the basis of conditions found.

Cash

In his reconciliations of bank accounts, the auditor should probably examine endorsements and bank perforations of all checks returned with the bank statement received directly from the bank. If the period covered by the statement is a short one or if the bookkeeper does not examine these details in monthly bank account reconciliations, this examination should be extended to paid checks of one other month.

It is suggested that cash receipts and disbursements per the books be reconciled to deposits and disbursements per the bank statements for two months of the year—the month preceding the auditor's reconciliation and one other earlier in the year. For the same two months receipts per the cash book should be checked to prompt deposits per bank statements and the cash book should be footed, page totals crossfooted, and monthly postings checked to the general ledger.

For the period from June 27 to approximately July 10 cash receipts as recorded in the books should be traced to prompt deposits per bank statements, and transfers between banks should be checked to determine that these transfers are received and disbursed in the same period.

Securities

Since securities constitute a material item in the balance sheet of the Putnam Lumber Company, Inc., and since they are not under good internal control, transactions during the year should be analyzed, brokers' advices examined for all purchases and sales, and securities on hand at the year end examined or confirmed with the holder.

Income from securities should be checked in detail—interest by computation and dividends by reference to one of the dividend services.

The balance sheet as presented does not show the market value of temporary investments. This market value should be computed and, if it differs materially from book value, indicated in the balance sheet.

Notes Receivable

Consideration should be given to confirmation of notes receivable. The balance sheet does not indicate their nature. If the makers are employees and the notes are being paid off through regular payroll deductions, confirmation may not be necessary, but if the makers are customers, 100% confirmation will probably be advisable.

Accounts Receivable

It is suggested that an aged trial balance of accounts receivable be prepared by the client and checked in detail to the accounts receivable ledger. Confirmation should be requested of all account receivable balances at or near the year end because of the relatively small number of customers. The negative form of confirmation request is recommended unless the auditor has a special reason for, or the client requests, use of the positive form.

Inventory

The description of the company's procedures does not indicate that perpetual inventory records are checked by physical counts. Assuming that the client checks perpetual inventory records, either completely at a date near the year end or by test checks throughout the year, the auditor may be able to satisfy himself as to physical quantities by checking counts of items accounting for approximately 10% of the money value of both raw material and finished flooring. This check should be extended if perpetual records are found inaccurate; it is probably inadvisable to reduce it to less than 10% even if early tests indicate that perpetual records are accurate. It is also possible that lumber, the largest if not the only item of raw material, may be so piled that a complete count can be made readily.

It should be pointed out that the checking of counts is only one step in determining the accuracy of physical inventories; review of the company's procedures for counting, and observation that prescribed procedures are being followed are frequently more important in determining this accuracy.

The measure of 10% can be applied also to (a) the check of inventory prices of raw materials to vendors' invoices and to quoted market prices, (b) the check of inventory prices of work in process and finished flooring to production costs, (c) the check of the inventory listing to perpetual inventory records, and (d) extensions and footings of the inventory listing. Summarization of the inventory should be checked in detail to supporting sheets, and footed.

Fixed Assets and Reserves for Depreciation

Since additions to fixed assets are usually in relatively large unit amounts, it will probably be practical to substantiate them in detail by examination of invoices and other cost records. Invoices should be examined for proper approval and for propriety of the accounting.

Removals of fixed assets will probably be few and, if material, can be checked in detail to recorded cost and to client's invoices for amounts realized on disposition.

A test check of the computation of 10% of additions to reserve for depreciation should be sufficient. Computation of charges to reserve accounts for fixed assets removed, if material, should be checked in detail.

Deferred Charges

Deferred charges are not material in amount. Unexpired insurance will probably be verified by a complete examination of insurance policies and computation of amounts unexpired at the year end.

Liabilities

Because of the weaknesses of internal control, consideration should be given to requesting from all principal vendors confirmation of accounts payable at the year end. The extent of examination of other liability accounts can probably be determined only after analyzing these accounts. It is doubtful that sampling will enter into the verification of any of them.

Capital Stock

No mention is made of a transfer agent or registrar so it will probably be advisable to examine the stock certificate book in detail. Transactions will be few, if any.

Income and Expense

An adequate program for the examination of sales cannot be developed without further knowledge of the company's procedures. The following program may prove sufficient—examine one large sale in each month of the year, tracing it to the customer's order, checking prices to current lists, proving extensions and additions, and tracing the total of the invoice to the accounts receivable ledger.

Dividends received, a material item of Other Income will have been verified as described under Securities above. Discounts allowed will be test checked in the examination of cash disbursements described below. Verification of other items of Other Income will depend upon analyses or scrutiny of the accounts.

Examination of cash disbursements for two months in the year is suggested: checking payments to vendors' invoices or other documents; observing approvals, propriety of account, and that cash discounts are taken when allowed; and examining endorsed paid checks for all disbursements.

Payrolls—The examination of a payroll for one period in the year may be sufficient. This examination will be in detail rather than on a test basis, since the number of employees is small and time saved by testing would not be material.

Consideration should be given to pay-off by the auditor of one payroll of the Realty Company. It is possible that employees may be so few in number that they are known personally to the officer of the parent company signing payroll checks, making a distribution by the auditor unnecessary. Since payroll checks of the parent company are occasionally distributed by one of the officer-stockholders, the auditor need not participate in a pay-off of the parent company payroll.

Testing generally will not enter into the examination of other profit and loss accounts. Verification will probably rely heavily upon comparison with accounts of the previous year and investigation of material differences in the two years.

Subsidiary

Since the subsidiary is wholly owned and its operations are material in relation to operations of the parent, consideration should be given to preparation of consolidated financial statements as presenting more accurately results of operations of the two companies.

ACCOUNTANT ''C''

Because there are many unanswered questions which an auditor would ask answers for and which would certainly affect my thinking as to the amount of sampling necessary on merchandise, I shall not attempt to outline the extent of sampling that would be necessary in observing the inventory. I would like to know how often physical inventories are taken and compared to the perpetual inventory records, what disposition is made of culls, whether the company has a night watchman present when the plant is closed, whether the plant is closed at noon, and who has the keys to the plant.

The decline in sales in 1955 should certainly be discussed with the officers/owners to determine if total decline is due to causes known to them. As I understand it, builders are not using hardwood flooring nearly as much as they have in former years, but rather are substituting cheap flooring and then covering it with carpets from wall to wall. Based on this thinking, I have assumed that the condition of the industry as a whole was such in 1955 that it was normal for the Putnam Realty Company to suffer an operating loss in 1955. If this is not the case, or if some other explanation for the loss cannot be found, the sampling, particularly in respect to inventory and operations, would need to be expanded.

I have also assumed that discrepancies in some of the relative operating expenses of both companies can be accounted for.

Unless so indicated the sampling listed below applies to both companies.

Balance Sheet

Temporary Investments—Stock (Lumber company only)

Due to the fact that this asset makes up a large percentage of the total, no sampling should be attempted. *All* stocks should be examined and scheduled in the normal manner.

Accounts Receivable—Customers (Lumber company only)

Since there are only approximately 50 customers, no sampling of this asset would be statistically sound. *All* receivables, except possibly those with very small balances, should be confirmed.

Notes Receivable

The information given in respect to notes receivable is inadequate to determine if sampling is possible. However, unless there are a large number of very small notes, they should *all* be verified.

Interest Receivable

All calculations should be checked.

Inventories

Pricing and extensions of all major items should be checked, and quantities should be checked back to the tally sheets. The listing, pricing and extensions of some of the minor items should be test-checked. The size of this test-check should be determined by the use of some statistical table such as Dodge-Roming table. (H. F. Dodge and H. G. Roming, *Sampling Inspection Tables—Single and Double Sampling,* New York, John Wiley & Sons Inc., 1944, 93pp). Accuracy should be such that we would be sure 99 times out of 100 that inventory calculations contain no more than 2 per cent errors. This sampling should be expanded if the physical count disagrees materially from the perpetual inventory records or if the gross operating loss is unexplained.

The Dodge-Roming set of tables includes several quality assurances, i.e., 99 out of 100. From these tables the size of the sample can be determined and the percentage errors in the universe can be determined by the number of errors found in the sample. The Dodge-Roming tables are merely suggested, as I am sure that there are other statistical tables which could be used for this purpose. Our firm has not been using such tables to determine the size of samples, but we are considering adopting their use.

Reciprocal Receivable and Payable

The balances in these accounts should be checked.

Fixed Assets

All changes in fixed assets should be checked.

Prepaid Items

All prepaid items should be checked.

Liabilities

All liabilities should be checked.

Generally, in the examination of assets and liabilities, it is not felt that any sampling should be done if there are less than 100 items involved or if there is a great chance of clerical errors. Sampling of a universe of less than 100, or of a universe that would be as heterogeneous as calculations of prepaid and accrued items, would not be statistically sound nor would the time saved by sampling small universes be worthwhile.

Operations

It seems that the company has as much internal control as an auditor usually finds in a small manufacturing company. There is a considerable element of control in the fact that each officer/owner can receive the mail, sign checks and that each has access to the safety deposit box. Certainly, very little need be done on the testing of cash receipts since practically all receipts are received through the mail and consist undoubtedly of checks and money orders. Little sampling is necessary on disbursements because the officers/owners have supporting invoices for each check signed. Also, the fact that the officers/owners are active in the business is very important.

The fact that the bookkeeper is a "good accountant" and well paid and that the plant is located in a small town probably minimizes the usual investigation for misapplication of funds.

Since there is a relatively small payroll and since it is likely that the officers/owners are personally acquainted with all employees, it appears that there is very little possibility of the issuance and cashing of payroll checks made out to fictitious employees.

It is therefore suggested that a check of one month's operations would be sufficient unless the test month reveals discrepancies that suggest further work.

ACCOUNTANT ''D''

Balance Sheet Accounts

All cash on hand would be counted, and that on deposit confirmed by certifications obtained from banks.

All temporary investments would be inspected and notation made of nominee if other than the company. Cost and market value of all of these items would be determined.

All customer accounts receivable would be the subject of positive request for confirmation. The accounts would be aged and details would be balanced with the control.

All notes receivable would be inspected and confirmation from the maker would be requested. Also, the nature of the notes would be determined, and their collectibility questioned. All interest receivable would be computed and checked by computation if accrued on the notes; if on securities, accrual from the last interest date would be checked.

Inventories of lumber would be observed during count by the company and the physical counts subject to a count as to one stack at least for comparison with quantity shown for other stacks. The quantity in the kiln should not exceed the capacity of the kiln. Cost should be determined, and the inventory pricing should conform with the company's consistent practice, and be compared with average market value by grade.

All accounts receivable from officers should be confirmed or otherwise acknowledged, and the amount due from the subsidiary should correspond with the payable on that company's books.

The capital stock evidencing the ownership of the subsidiary should be inspected and should correspond with the liability for shares shown by that company's books.

Real estate not used in the business should be the subject of an analysis and all deeds indicating title thereto should be inspected.

All deposits should be confirmed with the holders as to amount and purpose.

All fixed assets should be the subject of analyses. Title of the property should be inspected, and additions checked as being recorded at cost. Accountability for retirement should be determined and depreciation should be recorded at appropriate rates.

Deferred charges should be the subject of analyses and the correctness of the deferred portion of all items should be checked. Adequacy of insurance coverage should be determined from schedules and fidelity coverage noted.

Accounts payable should be compared with invoices and entries in the period following the close of the year.

Accrued taxes, both local and income, should be the subject of analysis and checked by reference to past tax bills and tax returns.

Outstanding shares of stock should be determined from the stubs of certificate books and the amounts stated for common stock and paid-in surplus checked. All changes in stocks since date of previous examination should be accounted for, as cancelled shares should be on hand equal to the new shares issued.

The foregoing procedures will cover the subsidiary for comparable items. The inventory of logs in the woods should be carried on a consistent basis with past practice, and inspected if thought desirable—logs in woods are not always inventoried and, if that is the regular practice, inventory may consist of lumber at the mill only and no trip to the woods would be made (assuming the mill is not located at the site of logging operations).

The farm account should be the subject of analysis and deeds should be inspected including detailed papers, as it was acquired during the year. In addition to work on fixed assets as referred to, timber rights should be the subject of analysis and contracts should be inspected covering purchases as to cost. The quantity of stumpage should be the subject of reports by cruisers and depletion should be checked from cutting reports. All notes payable should be checked from confirmations obtained and accrued payroll compared with the unpaid portion of the latest payroll. Deferred income should be checked by analysis and the item of rent collected in advance confirmed with the person from whom obtained unless clearly enough supported by contract which was inspected.

Operating Accounts and Transactions

Footings of the cash journal would be checked as to significant columns, i.e., discounts, freight and allowances, net cash receipts, net cash disbursements, purchases, etc., for three months and monthly totals crossfooted for six months.

Check postings from cash journal to general ledger accounts for three months.

Investigate any entries in general cash account originating in other than monthly entries from the cash journal.

Test allowances and discounts, freight, etc., and check the supporting documents to extent of two months' transactions.

Check from analyses prepared the income recorded from securities owned, real estate not used in business, farm rents, commission on vending machine or income therefrom, if owned, by adequate support for transactions for three months and comparative regularity of entries for remainder of year.

Compare canceled checks with disbursements in cash journal, examining all details for three months. Refer to vouchers for same period in support of all disbursements for over $25.00, noting distribution and approval and whether bills are marked "paid" to prevent duplication and investigate for an additional three months' period support for checks drawn to petty cash, payroll, and special payees such as officers, employees, banks, and others, which do not appear prima facie for purchases or expenses.

Inspect and observe regularity of bank reconcilements for the year and make "proof of cash" for the last month in the year and one other month by reconciling monthly totals of receipts and disbursements shown by the cash book with deposits and withdrawals shown by the bank statements.

Compare payrolls with disbursement record for three months and support two payrolls in detail by comparison with clock cards as to employees covered thereby. Inspect employment approvals as to all other employees.

Make a test comparison of copies of sales invoices to the journal in which posted. Proof of footing and posting should have been covered by work on cash journal but, if not, this step should be performed after details of invoices have been compared for the last month of the year and for one other month. For four other months compare total sales with reports of shipments for evidence of regularity.

Quantities of lumber purchased and sold should be approximately accounted for and if company records do not regularly do this, make test by adding to the inventory at the beginning of any month the purchases during that month independently totalled from purchase invoices and deducting inventory at the end of the month, then comparing the resulting quantity with quantities independently totalled from sales invoices.

A comparable step should be performed for the Realty Company, accounting for stumpage on a log scale basis compared to the mill scale used in mill quantities. Conversion from log to mill scale is by formula.

Footings of ledger accounts should be tested to the extent of about one in ten accounts and balances checked.

Analyses should be made of any expense account for which adequate support has not been seen in operations as outlined above, and support inspected if any appears desirable.

Analyses should also be made to obtain any information needed for the tax returns and not otherwise available. Notation should be made in detail of the status of examinations made by Revenue Agents of the companies' returns.

Minutes of both companies should be read for the year and to the date work is completed in the field.

A certificate should be obtained from the client stating that no liabilities, contingent or otherwise, exist to his knowledge which are not on the books; an inventory certificate should be obtained stating that the goods are the unencumbered property of the company.

ACCOUNTANT "E"

Preliminary Investigation

This is assumed to be an initial engagement. It involves a type of lumber manufacturing in which none of our other clients are engaged. We would therefore obtain, if at all possible, from Putnam's trade association group or from some other source, all possible cost, expense and profit data bearing upon this type of enterprise. Also, men assigned to the engagement and the supervising partner would be expected to familiarize themselves with available published material relative to physical operations involved in the Putnam enterprises or very similar enterprises such as pine lumber logging and milling operations with respect to which we have rather complete files.

Knowledge obtained in the above indicated manner would be supplemented by an actual inspection, as soon as practicable after staff members arrive, of the manufacturing plant and yard. This would be arranged at our request, before or after our customary office working hours.

The statements and explanations furnished by our Putnam clients indicate that we must rely to a very substantial extent on our ingenuity and auditing procedures to satisfy ourselves as to the fairness of the statements under examination, as a result, in part, of the absence of internal controls which might be utilized, but principally of the fact that substantially all bookkeeping and related record preparation work is of necessity performed by two persons in the same office. who apparently enjoy considerable latitude in the inter-change of duties and whose activities probably receive very little supervision or control by company officers.

Alert and somewhat extensive auditing is further indicated by reason of the importance of Putnam enterprises in relation to the small town bank where one general account is carried and the possibility that local bank tellers will accept almost any type of transaction suggested by Putnam's bookkeeper and cashier, including the reduction of deposits comprised of checks by the return of currency to the person making the deposit.

In formulating our preliminary program of auditing procedures to be applied, due consideration has been accorded the fact that both sets of statements to be examined are those of enterprises in which an estimated 80% to 90% of individual accounts receivable and purchase and sales transactions, particularly in respect to the Lumber Company, could be significant in relation to the stated net income for 1955. Also, the undetected falsification of only two or three accounts or transactions of the above mentioned nature could serve to conceal, at least until after the issuance of our opinion report, a material "cash shortage."

However, the relative significance of the above discussed accounts receivable (about 50 in number for Putnam Lumber) and transactions (estimated 300 to 600 sales invoices and possibly a 30% greater estimate for purchase invoices with respect to which less information is known) results in numerically few transactions, which can be examined for an entire year with less expenditure of time than would be involved in a two month examination of the transactions of, say, a wholesale grocer having around the same volume but more employees engaged in the preparation of accounting data and a generally adequate system of internal control.

For the reasons stated above, our tentative program, subject to revisions which might be indicated by facts developed as the work progresses, is as follows[1].

In actual practice, we would not attempt to outline a tentative audit program without more information than that shown by the case study under review. Therefore, considerably more discussion appears in text of the program than would be necessary or desirable under actual practice conditions.

The businesses under consideration are of a type in which fairly adequate monthly cost and income statements, expressed in both dollars and amounts per thousand board feet should be available. Under actual conditions, the availability of such statements and our studies thereof in relation to the drastic decrease in net income might

[1] Procedures apply to both companies, except as otherwise noted.

have a significant bearing upon development of the audit program.

If statements of the aforementioned nature are available, even on a quarterly basis, they will be carefully reviewed by the partner and senior in charge, both for the current and immediately preceding fiscal year, and a preliminary accounting made for the decline in net income. Operations for the two years will then be discussed with the management.

It appears from the nature of the lumber company operation that the major cost factors are raw material, labor and inventories and that the material increase in closing 1955 inventory despite the more than 50% decline in sales, will have to be carefully examined. It is also probable that the cash journal carries columns in which both lumber purchases and sales are recorded in thousands of board feet.

In any event, one of our initial steps will be to plan for a quick determination of board feet with respect to purchases, sales and inventories for the year 1955. It is known that production reports are available to account for flooring manufactured and for lumber produced by the Realty Company. Monthly totals of aforementioned accounts and related amounts per thousand board feet will be obtained from company records to the extent available and constructed by us to the extent necessary. Material fluctuations, if any, in both costs and sales prices per M will be reviewed with the management. For the purposes of this discussion, it will be assumed that logical explanations supported by limited tests of the records involved have served to establish a reasonable accounting for the decline in net income and for purchases, sales and the final inventory in terms of board feet. To the extent that board feet purchased, manufactured and sold have not been established by us from the best documentary evidence available, testing procedures hereinafter described will apply to both board feet and dollar amounts.

Cash Disbursements
(Except Footings & Postings)

General Bank Accounts

Examine all checks on general bank accounts, comparing with book entries and checking correctness of distributions to extent possible from information on checks. Ascertain that checks to officers and employees are properly recorded and can be readily identified in the test check of postings covered in another section hereof. As this examination is made, tick for comparison with totals of supporting documents all checks drawn to banks and for payrolls, salary payments, imprest cash and other payees which constitute the equivalent of a cash or bearer payee. Trace all checks to payroll bank account, other bank accounts and Putnam Realty Company to contra bank deposits. Ascertain validity and proper treatment in the accounts of all checks to officer-stockholders.

Undertake detailed vouching of all checks for last two months of year, making limited tests (about 10% of transactions) of calculations on documents supporting disbursements for material amounts and similar tests (about 5% of transactions) with respect to minor disbursements. See discussion under purchases relative to other work to be done as vouching is performed. This sample of documents supporting disbursements is deemed sufficient on account of the fact that officers make all lumber purchases and sign all checks. It is assumed that both officers are active in the business and work together in harmony; also, that checks are not signed in blank and that supporting data is inspected with reasonable frequency and, we hope, initialed as checks are signed.

Should our investigation and inquiries disclose the aforementioned assumptions to be in error, it might be necessary to extend the two month period, particularly with respect to checks issued for lumber purchases should numerous checks be found drawn to small operators who furnish no invoices for lumber delivered or should material errors be found in the footage accounting explained as previously established. Such lumber purchase checks as are not supported by acceptable vendors' invoices are to be identified with "tally sheet" receiving reports.

Obtain cut-off statements on all general bank accounts, to be mailed or delivered directly to us at a selected date subsequent to balance-sheet date, and have our staff reconcile such accounts and account for uncleared items as of the balance-sheet date reconciliation.

The test footing of cash disbursements is separately covered in comment on cash journal footings and postings.

Payroll Bank Accounts & Payrolls

Compare cancelled checks with related payrolls for the last two months of the year. Foot the payrolls (all columns) for the same two months and trace names to withholding statements on file for one payroll period. Trace hours worked to supporting time cards and time books for two pay periods. Test about 10% of net pay computations for the same two pay periods. Have rates of pay approved by an officer who is familiar therewith. Witness and control one pay-off for each payroll maintained, particularly with respect to those sent in by the superintendent of logging and sawmill operations.

As previously noted, transfers from the general to the payroll bank account were ticked for comparison with totals of supporting payrolls for the entire year. As this comparison is made, see that any unusual variations in payroll amounts are explained and that the number of payrolls corresponds with the number of established pay periods in the year. Ascertain whether employees have been accustomed to receive vacation or other bonus pay with respect to which liability accruals are indicated.

Obtain cut-off statements for payroll bank accounts at date of corresponding statements of general bank accounts and employ the same procedures as those previously indicated as applicable to general bank accounts.

The previously explained two month test of payroll footings should serve to accomplish the test footing of disbursements by payroll checks as it appears that the net pay column of payrolls would constitute the source of monthly credits to the payroll bank account.

Cash Receipts
(Except Footings & Postings)

Compare recorded deposits with deposits per banks' statements of general accounts for entire year and subsequent cut-off period ending with date of post-balance sheet statements obtained direct from depositories.

As to the Lumber Company Only (Paragraphs 1 thru 4, Below)

1. Account for dividends received by comparison of published dividend payments (Fitch or some other readily obtainable record) with analysis of dividend income as recorded in cash journal. This to be done for entire year.

2. The very substantial increase in bad debts must receive careful attention. With respect to all accounts charged off during the year, of which the worthlessness is not conclusively evident from correspondence files, obtain positive confirmation from debtors of record owing balances of $300. or more. Confirm 25% of charged off balances of less than $300. Also, review charged off balances and the possibility of unrecorded recoveries thereagainst with the officer having general supervision of credits.

3. Rents appear abnormally low in relation to the $83,000 investment in real estate not used in the business. Obtain a schedule of the properties which comprise this asset and establish rentals due to be collected from available records and discussion with the appropriate officer. Compare with analysis of rental income as recorded in the cash journal, *for entire year.*

4. Scan the discount allowed column of the cash journal for the last three months of the year to determine that entries therein represent approximately correct amounts computed on related gross collections, at company's established cash discount rate. For the last month of the year, trace collections of $300. or more to related invoices or customers' ledger sheets to prove that discounts have not been recorded with respect to invoices past due for discounting.

Both Companies Resumed

Since substantially all cash receipts are indicated as transmitted by mail, and are therefore presumably in the form of checks as distin-

guished from currency, and since deposits are made daily, the tracing
of individual collection items to duplicate deposit slips should not be
difficult. Make this trace for the first and last two weeks of the year
under examination and the first week of the following year. If duplicate deposit slips are not retained, compare daily totals of collections
from customers, as recorded in the cash journal, with daily totals of
credits to customers' accounts as shown by the control sheet in customers' ledger. If a control sheet is not kept, trace postings from individual customers' ledger sheets to cash journal entries for the last
week of the year.

It is assumed, in the absence of accounts reflecting scrap sales, that
such sales are invoiced in the same manner as regular sales; also, that
any sales of flooring or raw materials, for cash, are invoiced in the
same manner as charge sales. The examination of cash received from
sales of the aforementioned classes is covered in subsequent comment
on sales.

Receipts from sales of fixed assets, as determined from analyses of
property accounts, are to be reviewed with the company's officers as a
check on the proper recording of all property sold. Such receipts are
to be traced to cash journal entries for entire year.

Interest receipts are to be accounted for from schedules of securities owned, for the entire year. Interest on notes receivable is to be
accounted for from analyses of notes receivable accounts for the entire year. In connection with the examination of bad debt losses, ascertain from correspondence files and discussion with company officers, that possible interest collections with respect to charged off debts,
have been duly accounted for. See previous comment under "Cash
Receipts" as to scope of investigation with respect to possible unrecorded recoveries of principal.

Coca Cola machine receipts for the last four months of the year
are to be accounted for from purchase invoices showing numbers of
cases purchased for the machine and from the agreement covering the
amount of sales to be retained by the company for furnishing and
operating the machine.

The businesses involved are not of a type in which any

81

purchase rebates of significance would appear to exist. This matter is to be discussed with an officer, together with other possible sources of miscellaneous cash receipts. Account for such receipts, including sales tax compensation, for last four months of the year.

Sales

The internal control with respect to sales is particularly weak in that neither "tally sheets" upon which invoices are predicated nor the invoices are required to be accounted for by a printed numerical sequence. It is hoped that bills of lading required for railway shipment can be accounted for in a sequence of printed numbers and that the same situation exists in regard to truck shipments. If this can be done, a check of bills of lading against sales invoices for the last two months of the year would be sufficient to justify the belief that all shipments have been billed.

In the absence of appropriate records for making the above described test, sales for the last two months of the year are to be analyzed by footage amounts of each class of product sold and such amounts compared with credits to the perpetual inventory record of finished stocks. Also, if practicable, we would undertake a comparison of rail shipments with records of the local freight agents involved, for the last two months of the year.

As the above indicated tests are made, any sales for cash are to be noted for tracing into the cash journal. All footings carried to sales summaries in the cash journal and thence to general ledger accounts are to be proved for the above designated period. About five per cent of prices and clerical computations for the two month period examined are to be checked, the price verification to be made from price lists approved by an officer.

Purchases

Since checks are issued for lumber purchases immediately upon receipt of the lumber (with the same procedure apparently applying to purchases of standing timber) the previously discussed examination of cash disbursements covers a major portion of purchase examination. Also, some assurance as to the validity of recorded purchases of raw lumber has been afforded by the footage accounting hereinbefore explained.

In addition to the examination of purchase invoices for the last two months of the year, in the vouching of disbursements, the following additional work is to be undertaken.

As to Lumber Company Only

If board feet acquired are indicated in the cash journal with invoice amounts, the entries thereof will have been compared with footage billed in the vouching of disbursements. Otherwise, the invoices will have been set aside as vouched for the following work.

Compare either from cash journal entries of footage or from the invoices, the related entries of board feet in the perpetual inventory record; also, the unit prices thereof if shown by the inventory record. This comparison is to be made for the last month of the year to test the reliability of the perpetual inventory record. Under an adequate system of internal control, a week of such comparison would probably be sufficient.

Also, for the last two weeks of the year audited and the first week of the following year, compare purchase invoices with supporting "tally sheets" as to date of receipt and quantities. Trace the tally sheets to the perpetual inventory record. This comparison is to establish the reliability of the raw material inventory "cut-off" and the receipt of quantities billed.

Compare invoices from the Realty Company with the amounts of charges in its inter-company account with the Lumber Company, for the above indicated three week period, to establish the uniformity of inventory "cut-offs" of the two companies and the reliability of inter-company accounting procedures. Any differences in the reciprocal account balances are, of course, to be reconciled.

As to Realty Company Only

In the examination of disbursements, checks for the purchase of standing timber will have been noted for vouching. Analyze, the "Timber Rights" account and vouch debits and credits, including the inspection of footage shown by timber deeds, for the entire year. If the number of acquisitions "cut-out" during the year is less than 20% of the purchases involved, analyze prior years' acquisitions to establish "cut-out" leases approximating 20% of purchases for the year under audit. From the foregoing analyses, satisfy yourself as to reliability of the company's depletion accounting. If undue optimism in the assignment of board feet to rights purchased is indicated, adjustment of the balance-sheet valuation of the "Timber Rights" account upon the basis of the company's experience with "cut-out" leases is indicated.

Columnar Journal & Ledgers—
Examination of Footings & Postings
(Applicable to Both Companies)

Accounts to Be Tested

Trace postings from general ledger accounts to cash journal (and other records of original entry involved) entries and scan all entries to ascertain that no entries to accounts involved are omitted with respect to accounts as follows:

All cash and bank accounts

Accounts receivable—customers and others

All accounts of officers, bookkeeper and assistant bookkeeper (Include any accounts in customers' ledgers)

Inventories, accounts payable, notes payable* & notes receivable*

Putnam Realty Company & Putnam Lumber Co. (All intercompany accounts)

Complete above trace for entire year and prove footings of the accounts involved.

*Also analyze from notes held in paid file and independent confirmations of unpaid notes.

Perform the above indicated procedures for the last four months of the year, in respect to accounts as follows:

Sales, Labor, Inspection, Discounts Earned, Discounts Allowed, Purchases

Column Footings

Foot dollar amounts of cash journal columns in which monthly totals are accumulated for posting to each of the accounts and for the periods shown in the foregoing outline of Accounts to Be Tested, to the extent that such accounts are supported by cash journal columns.

To the extent that footings of cash journal columns have not been proven by previously indicated sampling procedures, foot and prove balancing as to debit and credit of all cash journal columns for the last three months of the year.

Except as to postings already checked, check all postings from cash journal to general ledger accounts for the last two months of the year. Ascertain that all recorded entries have actually been posted.

It will be noted from later discussion that the correctness of footings and postings reflected by additional accounts is to be established by analysis of the accounts.

General Journal

Scan entries for the entire year, which involve significant amounts, and examine supporting documentary evidence to the extent it has not or will not be inspected in the carrying out of other procedures herein outlined and relates to entries of a non-routine nature.

Prove debit and credit balancing or columns for the last three months of the year.

Perpetual Inventory Records

The extent to which these records are to be utilized in establishing their reliability, and in affording evidence to support purchase and sales invoices, has already been indicated in previous comment under the captions, Sales and Purchases. In the event examination procedures prescribed in the second paragraph under the caption, Sales, were not applied in the testing of sales accounts, such procedures are now to be employed if we find that the opinion report requested is not to be qualified as to the initial inventory.

Assuming that we are to assume responsibility for statement of the initial inventory and that the previously discussed "overall" tests of footage and prices produced logical results, the supplemental work to be done is described in the ensuing paragraph numbered two. In any event, we are to undertake the work specified in paragraph (1) below.

1.

Trace postings from daily production reports, and such documents as evidence credits to finished stocks, to the inventory record for the last month of the year. The records used to clear materials from the raw material account to the work in process account are not described. Trace entries on documents evidencing the original entry of such clearance to all inventory records involved for the last month of the year.

Prove clerical accuracy of inventory record figures for the last two months of the year.

2.

(If no qualification as to initial inventory)

Prove clerical accuracy of figures on 20% of perpetual inventory sheets or cards, using those reflecting highest dollar values, for the entire year.

Extend procedures detailed in first paragraph under "1" above to include January and June of 1954. Trace all quantities and unit prices, to the extent maintained, from perpetual inventory records to original records of the physical counts of stocks as of July 1, 1954, and of related pricing.

It does not appear logical that the Putnam Realty Company would carry any material inventory of logs not sawed into lumber. It will therefore probably have no inventory in process. In other respects, the examination of its perpetual inventory records, as previously noted, will involve the above described procedures. In providing such procedures, it is contemplated that all segments of the inventory records involve material amounts. With respect to any segments involving relatively insignificant amounts, the foregoing testing would be reduced about 75% unless the aggregate of such segments constituted a material factor, which appears to be highly improbable. A reduction of 50% in the prescribed testing would probably be warranted even if the aggregate of separate insignificant amounts should constitute a material factor.

Account Analysis

The following accounts are to be analyzed for the entire year—without reference to supporting documents in respect to (1) entries of $100 or less, except as noted below, and (2) entries in excess of $100 when adequate descriptive data does not require such reference, except as noted below.

Balance Sheet Accounts
(Including Purchases and Sales In Connection with Inventory Account)

Stocks—Examine support for all entries

Inventories and Purchases to extent separately recorded—Analysis to be limited to monthly totals of each class of debits and credits.

Sales—Limit to monthly totals as for inventories and purchases

The inventory and sales analyses are to include a reasonably accurate showing of numbers of board feet involved and may have already been completed in undertaking the board footage accounting hereinbefore provided. To the extent that such accounting might have established the accuracy of dollar amounts of postings and footings, the previously stated procedures relative thereto are of course to be curtailed.

Investments—Putnam Realty—Shows no net entries for year. Examine prior years' entries necessary to substantiate about 90% of the stated basis at which the account is represented to be carried. Any material entries offsetting each other during 1955 are to be adequately explained.

Real Estate Investments—Same procedure as Putnam Realty Investment, inspecting deeds and title policies instead of stock certificates.

Timber Rights—Extent of analysis previously explained.

Net Fixed Assets—Analyze for all asset accounts and related depreciation accruals, including items of less than $100 since relatively few entries are involved. This being an initial engagement, scrutinize ledger accounts, revenue agent's reports, disbursement records, deeds, insurance policies and title policies to establish ownership and cost of around 80% of dollar value per books. Reports of other reputable auditors may be accepted in lieu of substantially all the foregoing except evidences of ownership, in establishing cost. Make tests necessary to determine fairness of depreciation accruals and satisfy us that no depreciation is being provided in respect to fully depreciated cost.

Paid-In & Earned Surplus—Analyze all 1955 transactions. Scan major transactions of prior years to establish company's representations as to method of stating earned surplus, utilizing copies of income tax returns and reports of other auditors as a check on book entries.

Profit & Loss Accounts to Be Analyzed

Repairs; officers' salaries; office salaries; payroll taxes; general taxes, including entries of less than $100; legal & professional; traveling; rents; dividends received; donations; interest and gain on sale of fixed assets, in same detail as general taxes; and farm expense, the analysis of this account being partly to justify for tax purposes and partly to ascertain possible sources of income which might have been appropriated by officers.

Other Procedures
(Mainly Physical Inventories)

It is believed that, with the exception of physical inventories, the extent of sampling procedures to be employed in the examination of balance-sheet accounts has been covered in the foregoing matter. A possible difference of opinion might exist in regard to year-end balances comprising the accounts payable total. Our program in this respect, with the exception of fairly constant monthly obligations such as utility invoices, requires the substantiation of all accounts of vendors from which significant purchases are made, by satisfactory documentary evidence or independent confirmation.

Audit procedures involving no sampling, such as physical inspection of securities or direct confirmation of the holding thereof by others in the ordinary course of business practice, are believed as they relate to balance-sheet accounts, to be sufficiently well understood and generally employed to the extent that inclusion thereof would be undesirable for the purpose of this program.

As regards profit and loss accounts other than inventories the program hereinbefore outlined is intended to establish the reliability thereof with the exception of non-sampling procedures such as the examination of minutes, contracts, evidence of litigation or commitments involving material amounts, which are not considered to be within the scope of this program.

As to physical inventories, sampling procedures intended to establish the reliability of initial inventory quantities have been outlined. In regard to pricing, our examination would cover at least 85% of the final inventory value in view of the relatively few classes of stock and the significance of a great majority in relation to inventory totals. Assuming no material adjustments of the closing inventory to be required, examination of the pricing of around 70% of the initial inventory value would probably suffice.

In the absence of knowledge as to the previous reliability of perpetual records maintained and the limited degree of internal control in effect, we consider it essential that we be represented at the physical counts of final inventory quantities; also, that carbon copies of the counts be handed to us by the counters or that we retain custody of original count records until essential data as to total footages involved can be obtained therefrom. We would physically inspect all stocks of raw lumber and finished stocks and the entry thereof on count sheets. If the stacks do not vary significantly as to footage included (which should be the case) count of the pieces in 5% of the stacks and computation of the board feet represented is considered sufficient.

Lumber in the dry kiln is reported to be considered raw material and it appears likely that no paper record is made of quantities placed in this process; also, that physical inspection will not be possible. Therefore, it will probably be necessary to count cars outside the kiln on June 30th and obtain reasonable evidence as to total number of cars owned and normal loadings thereof. This should afford a basis for sufficient check of raw material in the kiln, when supplemented by examination of such paper record as is made to clear lumber leaving the kiln from the raw material inventory, provided our examination of the inventory in other respects discloses no material irregularities.

There will perhaps be some inventory of kiln dried stock which is to be checked as to quantities in the same manner as raw lumber.

Any supply inventories would probably not be significant but should be inspected to justify this conclusion and about 10% of the items of major value counted to check reliability of the company's inventory procedures in accounting for this asset. If any substantial quantities of readily salable items such as truck tires are maintained, adequacy of the physical and accounting safeguards provided against theft are to be examined.

Obtain positive confirmations from debtors with respect to year end accounts receivable balances of significance. As to opening accounts receivable balances, trace collection of around 25% of dollar value represented to cash receipts records and related duplicate deposit slips.

ACCOUNTANT ''F''

June 30, 1955 Fiscal Year Audit Program for Year-End Audit— Including One Interim Visit During the Fiscal Year

Cash Receipts

Check deposits per bank statements to cash receipts book for November 1954, May and June 1955.

Foot daily and monthly totals and check to summary journal entry for above three months.

Examine for unusual items and investigate in detail.

Review receipts in July 1955 and accrue June 1955 items.

For six days (June 28 to July 5) obtain, directly from bank, duplicate deposit slips and check to receipts book.

Schedule all bank transfers showing (a) date check drawn (b) check number (c) bank on which drawn (d) date deposited (e) bank in which deposited (f) date of clearance (g) amount. For November 1954, May and June 1955.

Cash Disbursements

Vouch cancelled checks for November, May and June into check register and note sequence of check numbers—examine voided checks.

List (a) double endorsements (b) checks payable to and (c) endorsements by officers and employees.

Foot totals for above three months and check to summary journal entry.

Review July 1955 disbursements for June 1955 items.

Banks

Reconcile banks (for November, May and June—Bank A; City Bank B; and Payroll a/c).

At June 30, obtain directly from banks standard confirmation form.

Obtain directly from banks statements and cancelled checks (from July 1 to July 12, 1955).

Petty Cash

Do a surprise count of the fund during course of audit.

Review petty cash slips for one month, noting (a) approval, (b) supporting data, (c) written in ink (amounts in words and numbers), (d) account charged is proper.

Investments

Inspect securities owned and schedule description and certificate numbers.

Indicate both cost and present value on schedule.

See that dividend income is properly received and recorded. Check to a security service.

Accounts Receivable

Obtain from client aged June 30 schedule of receivables also indicating collection in July 1955.

Review delinquent accounts with management, make necessary comments on schedule and set up adequate bad debt reserve.

Examine all write offs for executive approval.

Review returns and allowance subsequent to June 30, 1955 and set up necessary reserves for items applicable prior to June 30, 1955.

As of June 30, 1955, send "positive" confirmation to all customers—accompanying the regular monthly statements:

(a) Reconcile differences reported by customers.

(b) Schedule confirmation results.

Obtain certificate from client.

Foot the schedule.

Check approximately 50% of the accounts from the ageing schedule to the accounts receivable ledger.

Other Receivables

Prepare schedules and tie in to general ledger.

Confirm balance, if required.

List collection subsequent to June 30, 1955.

Foot the schedules.

Fixed Assets

Analyze fixed asset and reserve accounts.

Vouch acquisitions during year and determine propriety of capitalization.

Review repairs and maintenance accounts for items that should be capitalized.

Prepare detailed depreciation schedules. Note consistency of depreciations taken with prior years, tie in with reserves and depreciation accounts.

Prepare summary of fixed asset changes.

Prepare schedule analyzing profit or loss on sale of fixed assets.

Physically inspect additions.

Examine deeds and property tax bills to substantiate ownership of real property.

Inventory

At June 30, 1955 make substantial test counts of the physical inventory, scheduling the items inspected. (Count or inspect 60 to 75% in dollar value).

Check the items counted against the perpetual inventory cards and *final* inventory listing; schedule differences.

Request client to prepare duplicate adding machine tapes of the perpetual inventory cards and a duplicate copy of the summary of the tapes.

Prepare a price test schedule indicating the following for each item tested (account for about 50% of the total value).

    (a) Quantity in inventory (b) inventory price (c) quantity purchased (d) date purchased (e) price paid. (Examine sufficient vouchers working backwards from June 30, 1955 to cover quantity in inventory.)

For items sold in July 1955 compare inventory price with sales price for gross profit. Also for other items compare inventory value with last recent sales price.

Determine receiving cutoffs and check receiving records for June 29 and 30, and July 1, 1955 to perpetual inventory cards to determine whether all purchase invoices have been recorded and whether the inventory cards reflect the receipt of the merchandise.

Determine shipping cutoff and check to sales register and perpetual inventory cards to determine whether all sales have been recorded and whether inventory cards have been properly relieved.

Note whether invoices are being recorded in advance of shipment.

Examine truckmen's receipt to evidence date of shipment.

When checking to perpetual inventory cards, note and *list*:

    (a) slow moving and obsolete items

    (b) items which appear to be in excessive quantity in relation to use.

    Review valuation of above items with management.

    Obtain inventory certificate.

    Schedule commitments and note thereon any unfavorable prices.

Insurance

Prepare schedule of policies in force.

Vouch insurance charges and credits, post to schedule and verify accuracy of unexpired insurance at year end.

Check accuracy of compensation insurance and liability insurance invoices received during year and accruals at year end.

Review coverage for adequacy.

As at June 30, 1955, confirm coverage with broker.

Examine all policies.

Confirm officers' life insurance policies and cash surrender value, if any.

Deferred Charges

Schedule deferred charges.

Vouch charges to invoices, property tax bills, etc.

Check propriety and accuracy of deferrals at year end.

Notes Payable

Schedule notes, indicating rate of interest, interest charges and accuracy thereof.

Confirm by direct correspondence.

Accounts Payable

Obtain from client schedule of accounts payable at June 30, 1955.

Mail confirmations to all creditors with whom business was transacted in 1955, even if no open balance is reflected.

Reconcile creditors' statements and make proper adjustments and accruals.

Prepare schedule of unrecorded liabilities as at June 30, 1955.

Schedule results of confirmation.

Segregate items not properly classified as accounts payable.

Obtain liability certificate.

Check year-end accrual of expenses, professional fees, utilities, etc.

Taxes

Schedule and review all tax returns filed.

Note timely payment of taxes.

Reconcile payroll tax returns with payroll accounts.

Review State unemployment insurance merit rating and in connection therewith determine whether client is properly processing employees' claims for unemployment insurance.

Check year-end accruals of taxes.

General Ledger

Reconcile July 1, 1954 balances to June 30, 1954 accountant's report.

Analyze all balance-sheet accounts and selected nominal accounts such as: officers' salaries; insurance; dues and subscriptions; professional fees; taxes; etc.

Foot accounts and check to trial balance at June 30, 1955.

Check postings back to sales, purchase and cash books for November 1954 and June 1955.

General Journal

Examine all entries for year, vouching entries other than regularly recurring ones.

Check postings to general ledger for three selected months.

Review subsequent entries for items applicable to June 1955.

Capital Stock—Surplus—Minutes

Examine stock book and check stock ownership.

Analyze in detail all changes in surplus during year.

Obtain copy of all minutes during year.

Determine whether books reflect all matters pertaining to accounting.

Determine whether any footnotes to financial statements are required.

Agreements, Etc.

Excerpt, or get copies of leases, labor contracts, employment contracts, commission contracts, etc.

Sales—Sales Returns

Check prices to selected sales orders. (Take larger items on three or four days in 2 different months selected at random).

Compare shipping orders with sales invoices for one week in each of two months.

Foot additions of invoices for one month.

Check sales analysis for one month by adding invoices by type of sale, compare with summary journal entry.

Sales returns:

    (a) examine receiving report for the week ended July 2, 1955 and the week ended July 9, 1955.

    (b) determine that pricing is same as invoiced.

Purchases

Examine invoices and supporting documents for one month, note: (a) client is customer; (b) approvals; (c) receiving ticket; (d) date of receipt; (e) purchase order signed by authorized executive is in agreement with invoice as to price; (f) approval of price change.

Check extensions and additions of one month's invoices.

Vouch invoices in excess of $100 for one month to purchase book and to inventory cards; determine correctness of account charge.

Foot purchase book for two months (including June).

Payroll

Check time cards for two weeks, noting:
  (a) hours worked.
  (b) rate of pay (employee cards & union agreement).
  (c) computation of gross earnings.

Vouch two weeks' time cards into payroll book.

Compare payroll summary gross payroll with payroll book for the two weeks.

Foot payroll book and crossfoot for two selected weeks.

Compare signatures on receipts to form W-4 for the two weeks.

Check weekly and monthly summary into journal entry for one month.

Reconcile payroll accrued account at June 30.

Tie in payroll accounts from general ledger into quarterly payroll tax returns for the year under review.

ACCOUNTANT "G"

The audit procedures outlined in the following comments are intended for use in the Putnam Lumber Company, Inc. and its subsidiary, Putnam Realty Company, Inc. Certain procedures are more extensive in the degree of sampling than would be necessary in a larger organization employing a greater number of persons in the office. The degree of sampling will, of course, have to be extended if in the field examinations a high percentage of errors is found and conversely may in future examinations be reduced for certain items where a high degree of accuracy is found. The completion of the work outlined to the satisfaction of the auditor should enable him to issue an unqualified opinion.

Putnam Lumber Company, Inc.

Cash

Confirm balances as of June 30, 1955 with banks.

Reconcile bank balances with book balances.

Request that cancelled checks and bank statements as of a date in July (preferably after July 10) be delivered direct to the auditor. Account for deposits in transit and outstanding checks as of June 30, 1955.

Count petty cash fund and cash on hand (also inspect securities and notes receivable at same time) on date bank cut-off is requested.

Prepare a summary, by months, showing a reconciliation of cash receipts and cash disbursements as shown by the books with the bank statements. Reconciling items should be deposits in transit and outstanding checks at the end of each month. Any other differences should be explained.

Select two months for a detail test as follows:

1. Trace deposits by days to the bank statements.
2. For approximately 25% of the daily deposits, compare the detail per deposit slips with detail per books.
3. Compare cancelled checks with the record of checks issued as shown by the columnar journal, noting date, number, payee,

amount, signatures and endorsements. Obtain and check all supporting vouchers for checks issued in this period.

4. Foot columns of the columnar journal and trace posting to general ledger.

5. Any postings to the general ledger cash account during the year not originating in the columnar journal should be examined and explained.

Temporary Investments—Stocks

Prepare or have prepared a schedule showing description of securities, amount owned, certificate numbers, date acquired, cost and dividend or interest received in current year. Space should be provided for June 30, 1955 market values to be obtained from market quotations to the extent available.

All the securities should be examined at the lock box in the presence of either one or both of the officer-stockholders on the date of the cash cut-off.

Dividends should be checked by reference to a dividend record such as Standard & Poors or in the case of companies paying regular dividends by reference to current rates, or correspondence with the payor companies. This should be done for all securities owned on the first audit. On future examinations this may be reduced to a test check covering approximately 70% of the dividend income unless there has been a considerable change in the securities owned.

Cost and date of acquisition may be checked by examination of broker's statements of purchase. If this was other than a first audit, it would be necessary only to examine broker's statements for current transactions. In this case, there do not appear to be any current transactions.

Accounts Receivable—Customers

Prepare or have prepared a schedule of aged account balances as of June 30, 1955. Check balances on the schedule to the ledgers and the total to the general ledger control account.

In view of the small number of customers, a positive confirmation request may be attached to each statement and same mailed by the auditor. If the company prefers or the statements have been mailed, positive confirmations should be mailed.

The accounts should be reviewed with the officer-stockholders as to collectibility. In view of the large charge to expense ($39,672.66) for bad debts, the possible need for a reserve for bad debts should be discussed.

Accounts Receivable—Employees

Confirm the balances.

Discuss age and collectibility with the officer-stockholders.

Accounts Receivable—Other

The nature and disposition of the balance at June 30, 1954 ($59,972.56) should be ascertained.

Notes Receivable and Interest Receivable

Confirm the principal balance, due date, terms, interest rate and unpaid interest of all the notes as of June 30, 1955.

Examine the note or notes at date of cash cut-off. However, if there is a number of small notes, an examination of notes covering approximately 70% of the total amount receivable will be sufficient.

Test check the computation of accrued interest receivable.

Inventories

If there is a physical verification of inventory quantities, by the company as of June 30, 1955, the auditor's representative should be present and observe the manner and accuracy of the counts.

If it is the company's practice to use the perpetual inventory record as the basis for determining year-end inventories, the following procedure should be followed:

1. Check the physical existence of approximately 70%, in value, of the raw material and finished goods as shown on the perpetual inventory records.

2. By an examination of the receiving, shipping and production records for the period from June 30 to the date of the physical check, determine that the quantities as of June 30 are correct.
3. Examine the methods and procedures of maintaining the perpetual inventory records to be satisfied that they should, except for normal human error, correctly reflect changes in material quantities. (See procedure on purchases and in the same periods test 10% of the other postings to the record).

Under either method of quantity determination, prices, covering at least 50% in value, should be checked by examination of current suppliers' invoices and current market quotations for raw materials; and by cost computations based on the above raw material valuations, labor rates and current selling prices for finished goods.

The clerical accuracy of the inventory should be checked (a) by extending approximately 50% of the extensions and scanning the balance for obvious errors such as decimal points; and (b) by footing approximately 50% of the pages, scanning the balance of the pages and footing the totals (if there are no page footings, it will be necessary to foot the entire inventory).

Accounts Receivable—Officers

Prepare or have prepared an analysis of these accounts. Have the officer-stockholders approve the transactions reflected in their accounts and confirm the June 30 balances.

Accounts Receivable—Putnam Realty Company

Inasmuch as the intercompany balances are in agreement, an analysis reflecting the character, source and disposition of the intercompany transactions on each company's records should be sufficient to serve as a check of this account.

Real Estate (Not Used in Business)

Assuming this to be a first audit, we should examine documents covering the acquisition of this property. The documents should include:

1. Contract of purchase setting forth purchase price, date of transfer and other terms.
2. Warranty deed or quit claim deed containing a legal description by which the property can be identified.
3. Certificate of title, title guarantee policy or similar document.

If convenient, we should view the property as check on its existence and the use to which it is being put. If this is the source of rent, we should examine leases or rental agreements.

Deposits

Ascertain the nature of the deposits and confirm all of the June 30, 1955 balances.

Fixed Assets

On a first audit, it would be well to check the cost of the larger items set forth in the company's depreciation schedules. As to land, the same procedure should be followed as for the real estate above.

Changes for the current year, additions and retirements, should be analyzed and costs checked.

Prior year's income tax returns should be reviewed to see that there is a consistent policy as to depreciation and that book records and tax amounts can be reconciled.

Depreciation provisions for the current year should be recomputed. Reserves for depreciation and depreciation expense accounts should be reconciled and the provision in agreement with the audit computations.

Deferred Charges

Prepare or have prepared schedules of "prepaid taxes and licenses" and "unexpired insurance." Check the costs of all the items being deferred and test check the computation of the remaining balances.

Accounts Payable

Prepare or have prepared a schedule of accounts payable.

Before June 30, ask the bookkeeper to save month-end statements received from suppliers. Compare such statements with amounts shown on the records. Reconcile any differences. Examine cash disbursements for July and any unpaid invoices on hand for possible unrecorded items.

If there are balances not covered by the above and there is any doubt as to the balances, request positive confirmation from the suppliers.

Accrued Taxes or Other Accrued Accounts

Analyze all accrual accounts and make recomputations of balances due by examination of tax bills, tax reports, payrolls, etc.

Provision for Federal Income Taxes

Recompute the provision.

Accounts Payable—Officers

Ascertain nature of and disposition made of June 30, 1954 balance of $46,448.04.

Capital Stock and Surplus—Paid In

Examine capital stock records and stubs of certificates for record of ownership.

Check authorized stock by examination of Charter. The Charter and original State Franchise Report should be in agreement with the amounts shown for capital stock and surplus—paid in. Analyze and vouch entries in the accounts.

Earned Surplus

Prepare or have prepared an analysis of earned surplus setting forth profit and dividends by years and adjustments by years, indicating the prior years giving rise to the adjustments.

Sales

Compare total sales for two monthly periods with totals of duplicate sales invoices for the periods.

Check posting of approximately 50% of the invoices in each period to accounts receivable ledger cards.

Check the computations on approximately 10% of the sales invoices and scan the balance for the two month period. Include as part of this check a comparison of quantities per loading tallies and posting of same to perpetual inventory records.

Purchases

For the two months selected for a detail check of cash, compare entries charged to purchases with supporting suppliers' invoices.

Check approximately 10% of such invoices (scan the balance) for clerical accuracy and agreement with lumber tallies or other evidence of receipt of materials or services.

Check the posting of 10% of the lumber purchases for the two months' period to the perpetual inventory records.

Payroll

In addition to regular procedures on the payroll bank account, as outlined in the cash procedure, perform the following operations on payroll:

1. Select two payrolls in each of two months selected for cash detail check.
2. Compare time clock cards with time per payroll summary.
3. Check approximately 25% of the computations and rates as shown by the payroll sheets.

Inasmuch as earnings records are written at the same time as the payroll summary, it will not be necessary to check postings to the earnings records. However, cumulative totals on about 25% of the cards should be tested and compared to social security reports.

Expense and Income Accounts

All expense accounts in which charges or credits come from balance-sheet accounts should be reconciled with such account analysis.

Analyze, in detail, and vouch all tax accounts not covered by the previous paragraph.

Reconcile payroll accounts with amounts reported on State and Federal social security returns.

Analyze and vouch (to the degree shown) the following accounts:

Repairs (amounts over $100)

Repairs and fuel (lumber lift) (amounts over $100)

Auto repairs (amounts over $50)

Officers' salaries (check to minutes and earnings record)

Legal and professional (100%)

Traveling (amounts over $100)

Rents (100%)

Dividends received (see investment analysis)

Gain on sale of fixed assets (should be covered in analysis of asset account)

Life insurance (net)—What happened in 1955?

Bad debts (100%—Are all write-offs properly authorized?)

Donations (Have the company prepare a schedule and examine checks and receipts for amounts over $100)

General

Reconcile income per books and income per Federal income tax return for the year ended June 30, 1954.

Prepare or have prepared a schedule of income per books, income per original Federal income tax return, adjustments by Revenue Department, and income per adjusted Federal income tax return for the years ended June 30, 1952 and 1953.

Examine the corporate charter and the corporate minutes. Any items mentioned therein which have to do with accounting should be checked to the accounting records to see that they are in agreement.

A review of the statements raises a question as to the correctness and authorization in the reduction of officers' salaries in both companies.

Putnam Realty Company, Inc.

Follow the program outlined for the parent company as applicable with the following additional comments:

Farm (Not Used In Business)

Apply the same procedure as used for real estate of the parent company.

Fixed Assets

Prepare an analysis of the cost of timber rights and depletion applied. Vouch original cost and ascertain if there is any relation between timber rights and surplus arising from revalution of standing timber.

Notes Payable

Prepare or have prepared a schedule of notes payable as of June 30. 1954 and 1955, showing renewals, payments, interest rates and interest payments. Examine cancelled notes. Confirm June 30, 1955 balances.

Deferred Income

Check rent collected in advance by reference to lease agreement. etc. Examine terms of interest payments and compute amount shown as interest collected in advance.

Sales

Inasmuch as the sales of the Putnam Realty Company, Inc., are to its parent company, the parent company's purchases for the test period should agree with the subsidiary sales for the periods. Any differences should be reconciled and, if necessary, adjustment made.

Income and Expenses

The nature of the farm expense should be determined by analysis.

No provision is indicated for a claim for the refund of Federal income taxes due to the carry-back of the current year's operating loss. This should be discussed with the officers and appropriate adjustment or footnote made.

ACCOUNTANT "H"

Assumptions

We are to examine the balance sheets of Putnam Lumber Company, Inc., and its wholly-owned subsidiary, Putnam Realty Company, at June 30, 1955, and the related statements of operations and surplus for the year then ended. Our examination is to be made in accordance with generally accepted auditing standards, and accordingly is to include such tests of the accounting records and such other auditing procedures as we consider necessary in the circumstances.

For several years we have made annual examinations. The examination procedures proposed to be employed are based upon knowledge obtained from such examinations and upon the review of the system of internal control which has disclosed no material changes in prescribed procedures or the application thereof.

No bookkeeping work is done for the client.

Generally accepted accounting principles are being followed by the client.

We are to prepare separate reports on both of the above-mentioned companies as of June 30th and prepare the related federal and state tax returns.

We are also to prepare a letter of recommendations relative to suggestions for improvements in accounting procedures and internal control.

Putnam Lumber Company, Inc.

Internal Control and Accounting Policies and Procedures

1. Review the system of internal control and the accounting policies and procedures in use by the company and reflect all changes in the permanent file.
2. Prepare a memorandum on the weaknesses in the system of internal control and in the accounting procedures of the company together with suggestions for improvement thereof.
3. Evaluate the effect on the financial statements of any changes in accounting policies.

Tests of Transactions

With respect to transactions for two months of the year perform the following tests (with closer knowledge of the operations it might be possible to reduce these tests):

1. Foot the columnar journal and trace postings to the general ledger.
2. Reconcile total deposits for the test periods as shown by bank statements on file with total receipts as shown by the columnar journal. Schedule receipts by days and trace to the bank statements. Obtain explanation for unusual delays in depositing receipts.
3. Reconcile total charges for the test periods as shown by the bank statements to book disbursements as shown by the columnar journal. Check reconciling items by reference to canceled checks and other data.
4. Account for all transfers from the general bank account to the pay roll bank account.
5. Compare dates, payees, and amounts shown on canceled checks with data appearing in the columnar journal for the test periods. Examine signatures and endorsements.
6. Support propriety and classification of all disbursements over $50.00 for both months of the test period by reference to invoices, receiving reports, and other data. Examine for proper approval. With respect to lumber purchases compare prices paid with market quotations at the date of purchase.
7. For one pay period during the test period:
    (a) Foot the net pay column of the pay roll register and trace postings to general ledger. Compare pay roll checks to the pay roll summary for date, payee, signature, and cancellation date.
    (b) Select 10 employees in the test pay roll:
       (1) Support hours worked by examination of time cards properly approved.
       (2) Support wage rates by reference to rate authorizations.

108

(3) Test computation of gross pay.

(4) Review deductions for propriety.

(5) Examine endorsements on the pay roll checks and compare with signatures on the employment records.

8. For two weeks of the test period, one week from each test month, check the prices and eyetest the extensions and footings on sales invoices and compare to the sales column of the columnar journal.

9. Trace approximately 5%, in number, of the shipping tallies of the test periods to the sales invoices and then to the accounts receivable ledger cards.

10. Review cash discounts granted.

11. Select approximately 10 customers' ledger cards and compare postings to the sales invoices, cash receipts and credit memorandums. Determine that all noncash credits are approved by responsible employees.

12. Review debit and credit memorandums.

For the entire period:

1. Review all general journal entries for the period under audit and obtain explanation for unusual items.

2. Review general ledger accounts for unusual entries.

Cash

In Banks

1. Prepare or obtain and check reconciliations of the bank accounts at June 30th.

2. Obtain confirmation of the bank balances, direct from the depository, as of June 30th.

3. Request the bank to mail the July 31st bank statements, together with canceled checks and other data, directly to us.

4. Compare canceled checks returned with cutoff bank statement with list of outstanding checks as shown on bank reconciliations. Examine supporting data for old (over 30 days) or large (over $500) checks not returned with cutoff statement.

5. Trace deposits in transit at June 30th to the cutoff bank statement. Trace out all bank transfers for ten days before and ten days after the balance-sheet date.

6. Examine bank memorandums or other data in support of any reconciling items not cleared in above tests.

7. Review cash transactions for June and until the completion of the examination for unusual items.

On Hand

1. Count the petty cash fund and any undeposited receipts and reconcile from the date of count to the balance-sheet date. Examine petty cash vouchers for all amounts reimbursed in the period from the balance-sheet date to the date of our count.

Temporary Investments—Stock

1. Examine and list stock certificates in the lockbox at June 30th. Ascertain that securities are in the name of the company or properly assigned thereto. If the examination must be made at a date other than June 30th, request that no access be had to the box except in our presence and obtain confirmation directly from the bank that such was the case. Examine supporting data for transactions in the interim period, if any, and reconcile count data to amounts recorded in the general ledger.

2. Schedule any transactions in the temporary investments accounts for the period under review. Show details of dividend income and gain and loss on any sales.

3. Support all purchases and sales of securities by reference to brokers' advices.

4. Support all dividends received on listed stocks by comparison with published dividend records. Confirmation of dividends paid on unlisted stocks should be requested from the paying companies or other reliable sources. Reconcile to the dividend income accounts.

5. Reconcile gain or loss on sale of securities to the appropriate income or expense account.

6. Obtain market prices of all stocks. Consider an adjustment to estimated realizable value if market value is less than amounts recorded at June 30th.

Accounts and Notes Receivable

1. Obtain trial balances of all accounts and notes receivable at June 30th. Prove footings of total column and eyetest footings of aging columns. Review the aging of the accounts receivable from customers and investigate unusually large balances. Obtain details of accounts receivable from employees and others and of notes receivable and investigate old or unusual accounts.
2. Obtain the June 30th customers' statements from the client. Send positive confirmation requests on all accounts. Check names and addresses on statements to the other company records. Control mailing of statements and confirmation requests.
3. With respect to notes request direct confirmation of unpaid balance, interest rate, date to which interest is paid, collateral, etc. Review calculation of interest income and accrued interest receivable and trace to appropriate income account.
4. Obtain explanation for all exceptions disclosed by replies to confirmation requests. Mail second requests to accounts not replying to the first request.
5. Obtain a sales cutoff by comparing shipping tallies prepared by the warehouseman for one week before and one week after the balance sheet date with invoices, sales recorded in the columnar journal, and customer ledger cards. Also investigate returned sales. (See inventories.)
6. Examine credit memorandums issued in the month subsequent to year end for items applicable to the year under review.
7. Review past-due and unusual accounts with the officers and with the person in charge of collections and request that uncollectible accounts be written off.
8. No provision for doubtful accounts has been made by the company. Review the results of the aging of the accounts and the subsequent payments on old accounts with the management and

recommend a provision for doubtful accounts if one seems indicated.

9. Ascertain that the officers have knowledge of the accounts charged off during the year. Review files and consider obtaining direct confirmation of the balances.

Inventories

(Assumption is made here that physical inventory of all lumber and flooring is to be taken on June 30th.)

Physical Observation

1. Prior to the date of the physical inventory, review the procedures to be used thereon with the employees responsible for the physical inventory. Discuss such items as cutoff procedures, physical segregation, identification, movement during inventory, etc. Request any changes in procedures considered necessary to give assurance that the physical inventory will be reliable.

2. Arrange to have our representatives present on the date of the physical inventory for the purpose of observing the procedures of the company and for making test counts.

3. Check or eyetest counts of all items having large quantities or high unit values and about 5%, in number, of smaller items. Observe the procedures being used to compile the inventory and determine that instructions as issued are being followed. Obtain explanation for items not inventoried. Observe the general condition of the inventory for nonusable items and possible obsolescence. Watch for proper descriptions, particularly as to grades.

4. Review lumber tallies of receipts and shipments for one week prior and one week subsequent to inventory. Determine that a proper cutoff has been made.

Other Audit Work

QUANTITIES

1. Obtain a summary of the inventory at the balance-sheet date,

the inventory tags (or listings), and all reconciling data supporting the summary.

2. Trace all audit observations to the inventory tags and then from the tags to the summary. In addition, check quantities by comparison of tags to the summary and from the summary to tags until satisfied that a careful and reasonably accurate compilation was made.

3. Obtain evidence as to the existence of quantities for any inventory tags covering a high dollar amount in the inventory which were not included in the audit observations.

EXTENSIONS AND FOOTINGS

(It is assumed here that all inventories have been adequately checked by the client.)

1. Check or eyetest computations on 10% of the extensions in the inventory, including all items with large quantities and all items of high unit value.

2. Eyetest all page totals.

3. Compare the page totals to the inventory summary.

PRICE

(In the following tests no consideration is given to inter-company profits in inventories.)

MATERIAL:

1. Compare prices used in costing the inventory to invoices in sufficient quantity to cover the quantity in inventory on all items of total value in excess of $1,000 and about 5%, in number, of the remaining items. Care must be exercised in obtaining proper prices by grades.

2. Obtain market prices at balance-sheet date from published quotations or from latest representative invoices. Check about 10% of the items to determine that the inventory is priced at the lower of cost (presumably on a first-in, first-out basis) or market.

LABOR:

1. Review the company's methods of allocating direct labor to inventory and check the propriety thereof. For about 5% of the

items affected compare labor costs used in inventory to average labor costs per unit of production or for the period of inventory accumulation.

BURDEN:

1. For about 5% of the items affected check the application of burden to inventory as used by the company. Compare the burden rate used with actual percentage of burden to labor for the period of accumulation in the inventory.

2. Review the factors of burden for expenses which are not inventoriable costs but are chargeable to expense when incurred.

   (Note: An over-all conversion cost factor could be used to apply labor and burden to inventories. This, however, would not change the basic auditing procedures to be followed.)

SALES CUTOFF (see accounts receivable)

1. Trace shipments as shown by lumber tallies for one week before and one week after inventory to the cost of sales summaries used for relieving inventory accounts. Determine that sales have been recorded and costed in the proper period. This test can be performed in conjunction with the sales cutoff test included in the audit of accounts receivable.

RECEIVING CUTOFF

1. Obtain a list of in-transit materials, prove the footings thereon, and trace to the inventory summary.

2. Examine the invoices recorded in the month subsequent to balance-sheet date for material received or invoices dated prior to such date. Determine that all such items have been recorded or have been included in the invoices-in-transit schedules in the physical inventory summary.

3. Examine supporting information for all items on in-transit schedules in excess of $500 not cleared in test 2. above.

PERPETUAL INVENTORY RECORDS

(Apparently in this case these records control both quantities and dollar amounts.)

1. Compare inventory tabulations on about 10% of the items with perpetual inventory records and totals with general ledger

114

inventory accounts and investigate large or unusual differences.

OBSOLESCENCE

1. List all material items noted in the price tests for which no purchases have been made in the current year and all nonusable and possibly obsolete items noted in connection with the tests of the physical inventory.

2. Determine by review with management if any major production or product changes have occurred which render any inventory obsolete.

3. Review usage records and sales forecasts, and discuss with the management all items included in the tests noted above. Request that obsolete and nonusable items be written down to net salvage value.

TEST OF NET REALIZABLE VALUE

1. Compare selling prices on all major grades of finished flooring with the inventory cost and determine that inventories are not priced in excess of selling price less delivery cost.

Other Assets

1. Prepare or obtain and check trial balances of receivables included in other assets, such as officers, employees, etc. Confirm all accounts with the debtors. Check subsequent payments and discuss the collectibility of old items.

2. Request confirmation of deposits.

3. Prepare or obtain schedule of intercompany investment and receivable or payable accounts. Ascertain that receivable or payable accounts agree with similar accounts on the records of the subsidiary. Determine that the carrying value of the investment on the parent company's books is stated on a basis consistent with that of the preceding year and in any event is not in excess of the value of the net assets of the subsidiary company.

4. Prepare or obtain schedule of transactions in the nonoperating real estate accounts for the year and perform the following tests:

115

(a) Support all additions or disposals for the period by reference to invoices, deeds, mortgages, etc. In connection with all sales, reconcile the resulting gain or loss to the appropriate income or expense account.

(b) Check the ownership of the real estate by reference to tax bills, insurance policies, and county records or by confirmation with a local abstract company. (This check need not be performed every year.)

(c) Determine that the carrying value of the real estate is not in excess of a fair or reasonable valuation.

Fixed Assets

1. Prepare or obtain summary of property accounts and related reserves for depreciation, including the activity in the accounts for the audit period.

2. Support the cost of all major additions (over $500) in the current year by reference to invoices and other supporting data.

3. Examine supporting data for important sales and retirements during the period and compute the resulting gain or loss on disposals. Trace to appropriate income account.

4. Check the adequacy of the provision for depreciation for the year by use of an over-all calculation for each class of asset. Reconcile to depreciation expense charged to operations.

5. Select 50 major items of machinery and equipment from the records and physically examine the items. In addition, select 50 other items in use in the plant and trace them to the property records. Include in these tests all major types of equipment. (This test need not be performed every year.)

Deferred Charges

1. Obtain or prepare a schedule of unexpired insurance premiums at June 30th. Examine policies and agents' invoices and review computation of the unexpired portion of the premiums.

2. Obtain or prepare a schedule of prepaid taxes at June 30th.

Examine tax receipts or returns and check the computation of the prepaid portion at June 30th.

3. Obtain details on other deferred charges and determine whether they can be properly deferred to the next period.

Accounts Payable

1. Prepare or obtain and check trial balance of accounts payable at June 30th.
2. Review procedures for liability cutoff of expenses at June 30th (inventory items have been included in the tests of the inventory receiving cutoff).
3. Review invoices for the period subsequent to June 30th for items applicable to the period under audit.
4. Obtain independent confirmation of balances due from about 25 major vendors as at June 30th. Tie in balances thus disclosed with balances per trial balance and obtain explanations for exceptions, if any.

Accrued Liabilities

1. Obtain or prepare a schedule of taxes for the year and review as to reasonableness. Reconcile to appropriate tax expense account. Include full details of taxes paid for use in preparing the federal tax return.
2. Check the adequacy of the accrued pay roll by reference to pay roll summaries and other data.
3. Determine by reference to union or personnel agreements the requirements for vacation pay, insurance, and pensions and check the adequacy of the provision for such liabilities.
4. Examine Revenue Agent's reports for prior years and determine that all assessments have been paid or accrued. Check the computation of the current year tax provision.
5. Obtain details on other liability accounts and confirm or check as appropriate.

Capital

1. Prepare analyses of transactions in capital stock, paid-in sur-

plus, and earned surplus accounts for the period.

2. Examine stock certificate stubs in support of outstanding shares at June 30th. Determine that capital stock transfer tax stamps have been properly affixed to all shares transferred.

3. Check dividends paid by reference to the minutes of directors' meetings.

Operations

1. Obtain analysis of sales by product lines and compare with previous years. Obtain explanation for unusual increases or decreases in classes of sales.

2. Compare gross profit percentages for current year with previous years. Investigate material changes.

3. Obtain analyses or otherwise account for the balances in the following accounts:

Depreciation
Taxes
Repairs
Legal and professional
Donations
Bad debts
Interest income and expense
Rent income
Miscellaneous income and expense
Officers' salaries

Include full details for use in preparing the federal and state tax returns.

4. Review charges to repairs for major items of a capitalizable nature.

5. Compare income and expense accounts with previous years. Obtain explanation for all significant increases or decreases.

Miscellaneous

1. Brief the minutes of stockholders' and directors' meetings held during the year and up to the completion of the examination.

Trace all appropriate items to the accounting records.

2. Obtain directly from legal counsel information with respect to pending claims, judgments, and other litigation.

3. Obtain information from the management relative to expansion programs, and to unusually large purchase or sales commitments and possible contingent losses thereon.

4. Review transactions for the period from the balance-sheet date to the completion of the audit for unusual items, unrecorded transactions, etc.

5. Obtain copies of important contracts and agreements and incorporate them in the permanent file.

6. Ascertain that employees in position of trust are properly bonded.

7. Investigate adequacy of other insurance coverage.

8. Obtain a letter of representations as to receivables, inventories, contingent liabilities, etc., from the company signed by the officers and the office manager.

Putnam Realty Company
Internal Control and Accounting Policies and Procedures

1. Review the system of internal control and the accounting policies and procedures in use by the company and reflect all changes in the permanent file.

2. Prepare a memorandum on the weaknesses in the system of internal control and in the accounting procedures of the company together with suggestions for improvement thereof.

3. Evaluate the effect on the financial statements of any changes in accounting policies.

Tests of Transactions

With respect to transactions for two months of the year perform the following tests (with closer knowledge of the operations it might be possible to reduce these tests):

1. Foot the columnar journal and trace postings to the general ledger.

119

2. Reconcile total deposits for the test periods as shown by bank statements on file with total receipts as shown by the columnar journal. Compare receipts from parent company with data shown by records of that company.

3. Reconcile total charges for the test periods as shown by the bank statements to book disbursements as shown by the columnar journal. Check reconciling items by reference to canceled checks and other data.

4. Account for all transfers from the general bank account to the pay roll bank account.

5. Compare dates, payees, and amounts shown on canceled checks with data appearing in the columnar journal for the test periods. Examine signatures and endorsements.

6. Support propriety and classification of all disbursements over $50.00 for both months of the test period by reference to invoices, receiving reports, and other data. Examine for proper approval.

7. For one pay period during the test period:
   (a) Foot the net pay column of the pay roll register and trace postings to general ledger. Compare pay roll checks to the pay roll summary for date, payee, signature, and cancellation date.
   (b) Select 10 employees in the test pay roll:
      (1) Support hours worked by examination of time books properly approved.
      (2) Support wage rates by reference to rate authorizations.
      (3) Test computation of gross pay.
      (4) Review deductions for propriety.
      (5) Examine endorsements on the payroll checks and compare with signatures on the employment records.

8. For two weeks of the test period, one week from each test month, check the prices (by comparison with market quotations as of that date) and eyetest the extensions and footings

120

on sales invoices and compare to the sales column of the columnar journal.

9. For the same period as "8." above trace all shipping tallies to the sales invoices. Compare such sales with purchases of lumber by the parent company as shown by the records of that company.

10. Review debit and credit memorandums.

For the entire period:

1. Review all general journal entries for the period under audit and obtain explanation for unusual items.

2. Review general ledger accounts for unusual entries.

Cash

In Banks

1. Prepare or obtain and check reconciliations of the bank accounts at June 30th.

2. Obtain confirmation of the bank balances, direct from the depository, as of June 30th.

3. Request the bank to mail the July 31st bank statements, together with canceled checks and other data, directly to us.

4. Compare canceled checks returned with cutoff bank statement with list of outstanding checks as shown on bank reconciliations. Examine supporting data for old (over 30 days) or large (over $500) checks not returned with cutoff statement.

5. Trace deposits in transit at June 30th to the cutoff bank statement and any that relate to the parent company to the records of that company. Trace out all bank transfers for ten days before and ten days after the balance-sheet date.

6. Examine bank memorandums or other data in support of any reconciling items not cleared in above tests.

7. Review cash transactions for June and until the completion of the examination for unusual items.

On Hand

1. Count the petty cash fund and reconcile from the date of count to the balance-sheet date. Examine petty cash vouchers

for all amounts reimbursed in the period from the balance-sheet date to the date of our count.

Accounts Receivable

The company sells its entire output to the Putnam Lumber Company, Inc. Payment is made for all shipments upon their arrival at their destination.

1. Schedule shipments made for one week prior and one week subsequent to June 30th and trace the payment thereof to cash receipts detail and to the columnar journal. Determine that all shipments are recorded as sales of the proper period. Trace all such shipments to the receiving date of the Putnam Lumber Company, Inc., and determine that shipments in transit at June 30th were properly recorded.
2. Ascertain that the intercompany accounts agree with the accounts of the parent company.

Notes Receivable

1. Obtain details of notes receivable at June 30th and investigate collectibility.
2. Request direct confirmation of unpaid balance, interest rate, date to which interest is paid, collateral, etc.
3. Review calculation of interest income and accrued interest receivable, and trace to appropriate income account.

Inventories

(Assumption is made that the physical inventory of all lumber and logs is to be taken on June 30th.)

Physical Observation

LUMBER

1. Prior to the date of the physical inventory, review the inventory procedures to be used thereon with the employees responsible for the physical inventory. Discuss such items as cutoff procedures, physical segregation, identification, movement during inventory, etc. Request any changes in procedures consid-

ered necessary to gain assurance that the physical inventory will be reliable.

2. Arrange to have our representatives present on the date of the physical inventory for the purpose of reviewing the procedures of the Company and for making test counts.

3. Check or eyetest counts of all items having large quantities or high unit values and about 5% in number, of smaller items. Observe the procedures being used to compile the inventory and determine that instructions as issued are being followed. Obtain explanation for items not inventoried. Observe the general condition of the inventory for nonusable items. Watch for proper descriptions, particularly as to grades.

4. Review lumber tallies of receipts and shipments for one week prior and one week subsequent to inventory. Determine that a proper cutoff has been made.

Logs

1. The best procedures for taking a physical inventory of logs include the use, by the client, of independent experts to scale logs on hand at the inventory date. If the company does not contemplate this you should consider the necessity of retaining an expert to assist in your observations.

2. Observe procedures followed in estimating board-feet content of logs on hand at the physical inventory date, check mathematical accuracy and reasonableness of the computations, and make a record of quantities on hand for later tracing to the compiled inventories.

3. If cutting operations are to continue during the physical inventory period, ascertain that proper procedures are followed as regards costs incurred and logs cut. Ascertain that a proper cutoff is made by the company of logs transferred to the sawmill.

Other Audit Work

Quantities

1. Obtain a summary of the inventory at the balance-sheet date.

the inventory tags (or listings), and all reconciling data supporting the summary.

2. Trace all audit observations to the inventory tags and then from the tags to the summary. In addition, check quantities by comparison of tags to the summary and from the summary to tags until satisfied that a careful and reasonably accurate compilation was made.

3. Obtain evidence as to the existence of quantities for any inventory tags covering a high dollar amount in the inventory which were not included in the audit observations.

EXTENSIONS AND FOOTINGS

(It is assumed here that all inventories have been adequately checked by the client.)

1. Check or eyetest computations on 10% of the extensions in the inventory, including all items with large quantities and all items of high unit value.

2. Eyetest all page totals.

3. Compare the page totals to the inventory summary.

PRICE

RAW MATERIALS:

1. The cost of the lumber inventory to the company is the proportionate amount of the original cost of the timber. Review the cost data used in pricing the lumber inventory.

LABOR:

1. Review the company's methods of allocating direct labor (both cutting and in the sawmill) to inventory and check the propriety thereof. For about 5% of the items compare labor costs used in inventory to average labor costs per unit of production for the period of inventory accumulation.

BURDEN:

1. For about 5% of the items check the application of burden to inventory as used by the company. Compare the burden rate used with actual percentage of burden to labor for the period of accumulation in the inventory.

2. Review the factors of burden for expenses which are not in-

ventoriable costs but are chargeable to expense when incurred. (Note: An over-all conversion cost factor could be used to apply labor and burden to inventories. This, however, would not change the basic auditing procedures to be followed.)

SALES CUTOFF

Review the results obtained in the test of accounts receivable and determine that cost of sales has been recorded properly on sales for the period of one week prior and one week subsequent to June 30th.

RECEIVING CUTOFF

Review charges to lumber inventory for the period of one week prior and one week subsequent to June 30th and determine that all raw timber cut during this period as shown by production reports has been reflected in the proper accounting period.

PERPETUAL INVENTORY RECORDS

(Apparently in this case these records control both quantities and dollar amounts.)

1. Compare inventory tabulations on about 10% of the items with perpetual inventory records and totals with general ledger inventory accounts and investigate large or unusual differences.

OBSOLESCENCE

Review the results of the inventory observations and discuss with management the possible unsalable or substandard lumber included in the inventory.

TEST OF NET REALIZABLE VALUE

Compare selling prices on all major grades of finished lumber and determine that production cost plus cost to deliver does not exceed selling prices.

Other Assets

1. Schedule transactions with respect to the farm (not used in business) for the year and perform the following tests:

   (a) Support the cost of all assets over $500 acquired during the year by reference to invoices, deeds, legal documents, and other data.

(b) Examine supporting data on important sales and removals for the period and trace the resulting gain or loss to the appropriate income or expense accounts.
(c) Check the ownership of the real estate by reference to tax bills, insurance policies, and county records or by confirmation with a local abstract company. (This check need not be performed every year.)
(d) Determine that the carrying value of the real estate is not in excess of a fair or reasonable valuation.

Fixed Assets

Land and Depreciable Properties
1. Prepare or obtain summary of property accounts and related reserves for depreciation, including the activity in the accounts for the audit period.
2. Support the cost of all major additions (over $500) in the current year by reference to invoices and other supporting data.
3. Examine supporting data for important sales and retirements during the period and compute the resulting gain or loss on disposals. Trace to appropriate income account.
4. Check the adequacy of the provision for depreciation for the year by use of an over-all calculation for each class of asset. Reconcile to depreciation expense charged to operations.
5. Select about 25 large items of logging equipment and machinery and equipment from the records and physically examine the items. In addition, select about 25 other items in use and trace them to the property records. Include in these tests all major types of equipment. (This test need not be performed every year.)

Timber Rights
1. Prepare or obtain a summary of these accounts and the related reserves for depletion, including the activity in the accounts for the audit period.
2. Support the cost of acquisitions in the current year by reference to invoices and other supporting data.

3. Examine supporting data for any sales during the period and compute the resulting gain or loss. Trace to appropriate income account.

4. Review the computation of depletion for the period and trace to the appropriate expense accounts. Ascertain if depletion schedules reflect quantities as determined in a recent "cruise" of timberlands.

5. Discuss with management the present value of the timber rights in the light of potential production, marketability, etc.

6. Include in the working papers full details of depletion for use in preparing the federal tax return. Study the possible advantages to the company of Section 631 of the Internal Revenue Code and, if needed. obtain data on market prices required by that section.

Deferred Charges

1. Obtain or prepare a schedule of unexpired insurance premiums at June 30th. Examine policies and agents' invoices and review computation of the unexpired portion of the premiums.

2. Obtain or prepare a schedule of prepaid taxes at June 30th. Examine tax receipts or returns and check the computation of the prepaid portion at June 30th.

3. Obtain details on other deferred charges and determine whether they can be properly deferred to the next period.

Notes Payable

1. Obtain an analysis of the transactions in notes payable accounts for the period.

2. Review the loan agreements for pertinent items relative to the financial statements, such as surplus restrictions, current asset restrictions, collateral, etc. Determine that no liability exists as a result of default on any of the restrictions.

3. Obtain confirmation directly from the holder of the notes as to unpaid balance at June 30th. interest rate, date to which paid. collateral, etc.

4. Check the computation of accrued interest and interest expense for the year and reconcile to the appropriate expense account.

Accrued Liabilities

1. Obtain or prepare a schedule of taxes for the year and review as to reasonableness. Reconcile to appropriate tax expense account. Include full details of taxes paid for use in preparing the federal tax return.
2. Check the adequacy of the accrued pay roll by reference to pay roll summaries and other data.
3. Determine by reference to union or personnel agreements the requirements for vacation pay, insurance, and pensions and check the adequacy of the provision for such liabilities.
4. Examine Revenue Agent's reports for prior years and determine that all assessments have been paid or accrued. Check the computation of the current year tax provision.
5. Obtain details on other liability accounts and confirm or check as appropriate.

Capital

1. Prepare analyses of transactions in capital stock, surplus arising from revaluation of standing timber, and earned surplus accounts for the period.
2. Examine stock certificate stubs in support of outstanding shares at June 30th. Determine that capital stock transfer tax stamps have been properly affixed to all shares transferred.
3. Check dividends paid by reference to the minutes of directors' meetings.

Operations

1. Compare gross profit percentages for current year with previous years. Investigate material changes.
2. Obtain analyses or otherwise account for the balances in the following accounts.

   Depreciation and depletion

Taxes
Repairs and maintenance
Legal and professional
Donations
Interest income and expense
Rent income
Farm income and expense
Miscellaneous income and expense
Officers' salaries
Include full details for use in preparing the federal and state tax returns.
3. Review charges to repairs for major items of a capitalizable nature.
4. Compare income and expense accounts with previous years. Obtain explanation for all significant increases or decreases.

Miscellaneous

1. Brief the minutes of stockholders' and directors' meetings held during the year and up to the completion of the examination. Trace all appropriate items to the accounting records.
2. Obtain directly from legal counsel information with respect to pending claims, judgments, and other litigation.
3. Obtain information from the management relative to expansion programs.
4. Review transactions for the period from the balance-sheet date to the completion of the audit for unusual items, unrecorded transactions, etc.
5. Obtain copies of important contracts and agreements and incorporate them in the permanent file.
6. Ascertain that employees in position of trust are properly bonded.
7. Investigate adequacy of other insurance coverage.
8. Obtain a letter of representations as to receivables, inventories, contingent liabilities, etc., from the company signed by the officers and the office manager.

Index

A STUDY OF JUDGMENT CONSENSUS

AT DELOITTE, HASKINS & SELLS

Kenneth W. Stringer, Partner
New York, 1959

EDITOR'S NOTE: This selection, which I have titled for the purpose of this anthology, has been excerpted from pages 6-8 and 40-41 of: Gary L. Holstrum, 'Audit Evidence under Uncertainty: Empirical Evidence and Implications for Audit Practice,' presented at the Deloitte, Haskins & Sells Audit-SCOPE Seminar, Hyannis, MA, August 5-8, 1980.

A Study of Judgment Consensus at
Deloitte, Haskins & Sells

In 1959, Ken Stringer of Deloitte Haskins & Sells conducted
an experiment designed to test the degree of consensus between
auditors with respect to sample sizes selected for testing accounts
receivable, inventories, and vouchers. In this study, 92 auditors
(attending the Firm's meeting for in-charge accountants) were
presented identical data about the financial statements, internal
accounting control, the number of items in accounts, and the ranges
and distributions of book values with respect to certain balances
and transactions of a hypothetical company. On the basis of this
identical information, the auditors were asked to judgmentally
select an appropriate sample size for audit testing. The information presented to these subjects is shown in Appendix A. The
disconcerting lack of consensus in the auditors' judgments concerning
sample size is demonstrated in Exhibit 1.

Exhibit 1

Responses to DH&S Study - 1959

		Number of Items to be Tested			
Nature of Test	Total Number of Items	Range of Replies		Lower and Upper 10% of Replies	
		Low	High	Low	High
Confirmation of accounts receivable:					
Good internal control	2,000	50	600	100	500
Bad internal control	2,000	100	1400	200	1000
Test of inventory prices	5,000	25	1250	50	1000
Test of vouchers to "afford satis-factory evidence of internal control"	12,000	25	1000	50	1000

135

Disregarding the extreme replies, it may be observed from Exhibit 1 that the range between the lower and upper 10% of the replies, expressed as a percentage of the total number of items, was: from 5% to 25% for the confirmation of receivables with good control, and 10% to 50% with bad control; from 1% to 20% for the test of inventory prices; and from 0.4% to 8.3% for the test of vouchers. Expressed differently, the ratio of the upper to the lower 10% of replies was 5 to 1 as to receivables and 20 to 1 as to inventory and vouchers.

3

APPENDIX A

DELOITTE HASKINS & SELLS STUDY-1959

DATA CONCERNING SURVEY
AT 1959 MEETING OF IN-CHARGE ACCOUNTANTS

INSTRUCTIONS

This questionnaire is designed to contribute to our study
of the problem concerning the extent of audit tests by obtaining
a cross-section of the views and practices of our in-charge
accountants. It need not be signed. Please answer all questions
specifically and as promptly as possible.

The questions pertain to an examination of the following
condensed hypothetical financial statements:

Balance Sheet

Current Assets:		Current Liabilities:	
Cash	$ 1,900,000	Notes payable	$ 1,000,000
Receivables	3,000,000	Accounts payable	2,000,000
Inventories	5,000,000	Accrued liabilities	1,000,000
Prepaid expenses	100,000	Total	4,000,000
Total	10,000,000	Capital stock	10,000,000
Property - net	15,000,000	Retained earnings	11,000,000
Total	$25,000,000	Total	$25,000,000

Statement of Income

Net Sales		$30,000,000
Cost and Expenses:		
Cost of Sales	$20,000,000	
Selling and general expenses	4,000,000	24,000,000
Income before Income Tax		6,000,000
Income Tax		3,000,000
Net Income		$ 3,000,000

It is to be assumed that all items investigated in connection with the analytic review have been cleared satisfactorily.

137

4

ACCOUNTS RECEIVABLE

QUESTIONS

1. The receivables include 2,000 accounts whose balances
   range from small amounts to a maximum of $5,000, with
   no particular concentration of balances at any level.
   There are no accounts that appear to be especially
   old or otherwise unusual, and the internal control is
   good with respect to cash receipts, sales, and receivables. State the total number of accounts you
   would select for confirmation and indicate briefly
   how you would select them.

2. What changes, if any, would you make in your answers to
   Question 1 if internal control over cash receipts,
   sales, and receivables were bad, but previous audits
   had not revealed material errors in the receivables?

INVENTORY

3. The physical inventory includes 5000 line items, the
   extensions of which range from small amounts to a
   maximum of $5,000, with no particular concentration
   of amounts at any level. Perpetual inventory records
   show quantities and unit prices but they are not
   under general ledger control. The gross profit rate
   did not vary significantly from that of the preceding
   year. Inventory prices have not been rechecked by
   the client. How many items would you select for your
   test of inventory prices?

VOUCHERS

4. Your inquiries concerning the preparation and approval
   of vouchers indicates that internal control is good.
   The client issues approximately 1,000 vouchers each
   month. How many vouchers would you examine to "afford
   satisfactory evidence of internal control" in this
   respect?

138

AUDITORS' SAMPLING BEHAVIOR:
AN EMPIRICAL STUDY

William R. Kinney, Jr. & Blaine A. Ritts

The use of statistical sampling by auditors has been widely discussed in the academic and professional literature.[1] Most of this discussion has been at the a priori level considering topics such as the alleged advantages of the use of the relatively objective statistical sampling,[2] the applicability (inapplicability) of various sampling techniques[3] and the use of Bayesian analysis and judgment in sampling.[4]

Many of these articles report on ad hoc experience of accounting firms with respect to the effectiveness of statistical sampling. These experiences seem to indicate that audit time savings accrue to the users of statistical sampling due to smaller sample sizes than are normally thought necessary with the use of "judgmental" methods.[5] The same conclusion is reached after a more extensive empirical analysis by Aly and Duboff.[6] In addition, at least one leading auditing text supports this view.[7]

While the audit implementation of statistical sampling is apparently still in its formative stages, knowledge of the present state of implementation should be useful.[8] The purpose of this paper is to present results of an empirical investigation into the extant sampling behavior of practicing auditors applying methods which they would ordinarily apply in an audit context. The experimental setting is an audit case requiring the design of a "variable" (dollar value) estimation sampling plan. The case was administered to a group of practicing seniors of "Big 8" public accounting firms.

The Audit Sampling Environment

In making detailed substantive tests[9] of a given population the auditor must choose which items (or choose how to select a given class of items) to be examined. Only two states of the client's reported data are relevant to the auditor: (S_1) the client's reported data are "correct", and (S_2) the client's reported data are "materially" in error. Whether using judgmental or statistical sampling techniques, the auditor faces two types of potential error: 1) rejecting the client's reported data when S_1 is true and 2) accepting the client's reported data when S_2 is true. One way to reduce the probabilities of Type I and Type II errors (α and β) is to increase the sample size[10] and thus the cost of obtaining audit evidence. In making audit planning decisions, the auditor chooses the sample size so as to minimize the expected total audit cost by joint consideration of the   costs of Type I and II errors given that the errors have occurred, α, β and the sampling cost function.[11]

All auditors face the problem of obtaining "sufficient competent evidential matter" (to meet generally accepted auditing standards). Competitive pressures imposed by other practioners provides an upper limit on audit resources which can be devoted to a particular audit area. Since all auditors must meet the same standards, the question of the relative efficiency of extant audit technology naturally arises. Specifically do ex ante sample sizes differ among practicing auditors in a given situation, and if so, are the differences related to the measurable characteristics of the auditors? In attempting to answer these questions, ex ante sample sizes will be compared directly.

The sampling and auditing literature suggests that sample size differences in a particular audit context are likely to be related to differences in:

1. perceptions of the amount of a material error in the context,

2. perceptions of the adequacy of internal control in the context,

3. differences in estimates of the variance of the (audited) population,

4. level of experience and degree of skill in the use of statistical sampling possessed by the auditor,

5. (accounting) firm policy with respect to sampling, sampling plans or policies with respect to α and β given an internal control system.

6. differences in sampling methods chosen (statistical vs. judgment, stratified vs. nonstratified, protective vs. nonprotective[12], mean-per-unit vs. ratio or difference estimates)[13]

In conducting tests of association, then, these factors must be controlled or otherwise accounted for in the experiment. Within the context of a specific audit case, the last three factors were chosen as independent variables and by administering the single audit case we attempted to hold factors 1, 2, and 3 constant.

Factors 4 and 5 are, of course, likely to influence the senior's basic decision as to whether to use a statistical method. While it is possible to select subjects with respect to characteristics four and five, it is not possible to classify a subject as to method(s) until the subject indicates his/her sampling plan. Furthermore, particular method-factor combinations may not exist in practice or the sample. Therefore, our statistical analysis is based on a general least-squares solution rather than a factorial analysis of variance.

The Independent Variables

In a survey of practicing CPAs, Ross, Hoyt and Shaw have reported that the extent of training and experience in the use of statistical sampling is positively related to the use of sampling.[14] Further, they report that their respondents' cited lack of training and experience with the use of statistical sampling as the primary reason statistical sampling is not more widely used. This apparent lack of familiarity with the use of statistical sampling is also cited by others.[15]

An appropriate executive in each CPA firm was asked to select five seniors from among those in their office who were most experienced in the use of statistical sampling in auditing and five from among those seniors least experienced in such use (with the seniors' other characteristics as nearly the same as possible). This classification is taken as a surrogate for a senior's experience and skill in the use of statistical sampling.

With respect to factor 5, large differences among firms as to the percentage of jobs in which statistical sampling is used has been reported in a study of Los Angeles CPA firms.[16] Two big eight firms offices reported that they used statistical sampling on only from 1% to 2% of their audits while two firms reported 5%, one 10% to 20%, and one each reported 60%, 75%, and 100%.

Two empirical studies of auditors' reports on accounting method changes provide further indication of differences among CPA firms with respect to audit behavior (and therefore possibly sampling behavior).[17] In a study of auditors' reports concerning changes to accelerated depreciation in 1954 and investment tax credit in 1964, Neumann found that the Big 8 firms varied in the percent of reports with consistency qualifications from 7% to 47% (average 15%). Gosman selected 100 firms at random from 500 of the largest firms and determined the frequency of consistency exceptions reported from 1959-1968. He found that the percentage of clients which reported at least one consistency exception ranged from 28.5% to 87.5%

(average 63%) among the Big 8 CPA firms. As both authors note, there are various explanations for such behavior differences--one of which is differences in basic accounting firm philosophy as to evidence (both in amount and means of obtaining it).

Thus, firm differences are expected due to method choice as well as possible differences in audit technology and philosophy among firms.

The literature relative to the size of samples experienced in practice supports the hypothesis that statistically determined sample sizes are smaller than judgment samples.[18] In the only controlled empirical study concerning this hypothesis, Aly and Duboff found support for this claim.[19] They compared sample sizes determined by practicing auditors using judgmental sampling against researcher-determined sample sizes using (stratified) statistical sampling. They conclude that the application of statistical sampling procedures produces significantly smaller sample sizes than does the use of judgmental procedures. Since the implementation of statistical sampling by auditors may be far different from that of an academic researcher, the question of relative sample sizes chosen by practicing auditors applying methods that they would ordinarily use in a particular audit context has not been approached.

Based on these published results and claims it would be expected that statistically selected sample sizes prepared by practicing auditors would be smaller than those of judgmental samplers.[20] By implication, the same direction would be expected for the experienced/skilled in statistical sampling group and by auditors employed by firms which encourage or require the use of statistical methods.

The use of stratification has long been applied by auditors--auditors have traditionally sampled more heavily from the larger dollar value and/or less well-controlled items, other things equal. The audit case employed in the present study provided a natural stratification basis on product type (dollar values between product types were only slightly overlapping). Since stratified sampling plans rarely result in ex ante sample sizes which are larger than those selected on an unrestricted random basis, one would expect that auditors relying on stratification would have smaller average sample sizes than those not relying on stratification.[21] Stratified sampling plans were operationally defined as those calling for a different percentage of items to be selected from different product groups or dollar value group in which the maximum percent selected from any stratum was less than 100%.

The protection objective of the auditor in sampling is discussed by Ijiri and Kaplan.[22] A protective sampler selects large dollar value items (ignoring expected error rates) to verify as large a portion of the total account value as possible given a fixed sample size. The "protection" would presumably increase the auditor's subjective confidence in the reported balances more than would the same number of observations selected on some other basis. Since an economic auditor tries to obtain sufficient competent evidential matter at minimum cost, one would expect that the protective samplers' samples would be smaller on the average than those of the non-protective samplers, other things equal. For this study, a senior whose sampling plan called for the selection of all the items in the highest dollar value class was operationally defined as a protective sampler.

Thus, each senior was classified as being in one of two experi-
ence/skill class, one of six Big 8 firms,[23] one of two sampling method
classes (judgmental or statistical), one of two classes each with respect
to stratification, protection and mean-per-unit or ratio or difference
estimates.

The Case

An audit case was developed describing the financial characteristics
of Johns Plumbing Supply, Inc. (JPS). A detailed description of this
wholesale distributor's inventory of 1) plumbing fixtures (250 line items),
and 2) pipe and fittings (1,250 line items) and internal control system
was presented. The basic requirement was for the senior to indicate the
plan he/she would follow to select items for inventory pricing tests.
Application of statistical sampling to inventory pricing tests is straight-
forward and is a common application in practice.[24]

The two basic product types with different average dollar values and
relative variances provided a natural stratification basis. The internal
control system was such that any errors in inventory reported would be due
to pricing errors rather than count errors. This allowed the substitution
of the materiality of an inventory error as the pricing error which the
auditor wants to be able to detect via sampling. Also the internal control
system and business activity was such that prior year's experience was
likely to continue.

Based upon the information presented in the audit case each senior
was asked to sequentially complete two questionnaires (Form A and Form B).
The primary requirements on Form A was the preparation of an audit program
to be followed by an audit assistant in selecting inventory line items for
appropriate pricing tests to be carried out on the inventory of JPS and

the auditor's judgment as to the dollar amount of an error in inventory which would be considered material. They were asked to complete Form A as if they were actually planning the audit of JPS. They were also asked to evaluate JPS inventory pricing procedures relative to that of similar firms in the subject's experience.

Form B contained questions concerning the probabilities of Type I and Type II errors given the subject's sampling plan. Form B was sealed and the seniors were asked to complete Form A before opening Form B to avoid sensitization with respect to statistical sampling. It was felt that the nature of the questions on the second response form relating to Type I and Type II errors might motivate respondents to use statistical methods when they otherwise would have followed a judgmental approach. Responses to Form B allowed a determination of perceptions of α and β as well as further clarification as to the means used to derive the sampling plan on Form A. These questions allow some assessment of the consistency of answers within subjects and the consistency with which seniors understood the case situation.

The Empirical Testing

Large midwestern offices of the eight largest public accounting firms were asked to participate by distributing the case packets to ten audit seniors each. Six of the firms eventually responded in sufficient numbers. Fifty usable responses were returned by the subjects.

The sampling methods used in the audit plan were determined. Seniors who did not use sample size formulas or tables were considered to be judgmental samplers. Only one of the seniors using statistical sampling applied a Neyman (optimum) allocation to the stratified population and none

146

of the fifty used ratio or difference estimates eventhough each would likely be beneficial in this circumstance.[25] This may indicate a lack of statistical knowledge on the part of even the more knowledgable seniors.[26]

The average material error indicated by the seniors ($\overline{E}$) was 6.2% of net income before taxes. This is approximately equal to the 7% "average dividing line" between material and non-material errors reported by national CPAs in a survey by Woosley.[27] Average α and β were 6.4% and 7.5% respectively with 90% of the subjects indicating each less than or equal to 10%. Thus, we assume the effects of Factors 1-3 to be negligible.

Since only an audit program or plan was asked for, the required information did not necessarily include the sample size but could merely describe a way of determining it -- via formula and the parameter estimates from the case and responses or via a strategy based on other characteristics of the population (such as "select all line items with a reported total value of $2,500 or above and 10% of the line items with reported total values below $2,500"). Thus sample sizes were computed (or copied) from the responses.

For the statistical samplers who specified a "confidence interval" approach (and this included all of those using statistical sampling) but who did not specify precision, desired precision was set equal to the amount of a material inventory error,E. This generally implies $\beta = .5$ which yields smaller sample size than for $\beta < .5$, eventhough it may be far from optimal when the relatively large cost of a Type II error is considered.[28] Costs of errors and sampling were not specified in the case and therefore following a classical approach, sample size depends solely on α, β, and $\delta = E/\sigma$. For JPS, $\overline{E}$ per unit reported by the seniors was quite small relative to σ ($\delta=.04$) and therefore large sample sizes are required. Eight statistical samplers indicated or implied sample sizes of greater than 400 compared with only two of the judgmental samplers.

It may be that when the audit assistant computed the sample size indicated by the program that the statistical sampling senior would convert to judgmental methods. In fact, one explanation of the relatively small differences attributed to the experience/skill variable (described below) is that those skilled seniors recognized the large sample sizes required in the JPS case and converted to judgmental procedures. If such switching to judgmental methods did take place, serious question is raised concerning the arguments given by those who claim that "objectivity" is a primary advantage of the use of "classical" statistical sampling methods in auditing. Objectivity in some cases may be acquired only at the cost of larger sample sizes.

The Statistical Model and Test Results

The basic statistical model assumed was:

$$Y_j = \sum_{i=0}^{10} B_i X_{ij} + e_j,$$

where: Y_j is the sample size indicated by the j th senior,

B_i is the regression coefficient relating X_i to sample size,

X_{ij} is a "dummy" variable indicating the membership of senior j (or j's sampling plan) in a class:

$X_{oj} = 1$,

$X_{1j} = 1$ if senior j is experienced in the use of statistical sampling,
$= 0$ otherwise,

for i = 2 through 6:

$X_{ij} = 1$ if senior j is employed by firm i,
$= 0$ otherwise,

$X_{7j} = 1$ if senior j used a statistical sampling plan,
$= 0$ otherwise,

$X_{8j} = 1$ if senior j used a stratified sampling plan,
$= 0$ otherwise,

$X_{9j} = 1$ if senior j used a protective sampling plan,
$= 0$ otherwise, and

$X_{10j} = 1$ if senior j was experienced with the use of statistical sampling and used statistical sampling in the indicated sampling plan,
$= 0$ otherwise.[29]

e_j is the unexplained residual for senior j, and

$e_j \sim \text{NID } (0, \sigma^2)$.

A preliminary analysis indicated that the surrogate for experience with the use of statistical sampling (X_1), and the use of stratified (X_8) of protective sampling plans (X_9) and experience X statistical method interaction (X_{10}) did not explain significant variation in sample size even at the .1 level.

Differences in sample size associated with firm membership and the use of statistical sampling were significant at the .01 level. In fact, the hypothesis that average sample sizes for judgemental samplers was <u>greater than or equal to</u> average sample sizes for statistical samplers could be rejected at the .01 level. An abbreviated analysis of variance for the reduced model:

$$Y_j = B_o X_{oj} + \sum_{i=2}^{6} B_i X_{ij} + B_7 X_{7j} + e_j$$

in presented in figure 1. Figure 2 presents the estimated values for each factor combination, the actual mean and the number of seniors in each combination.

The average sample sizes per firm ranged from 83 line items to 388 line items, or 4.7 times as many -- from the offices of two Big 8 firms in the same city. There seem to be considerable differences in average experience in the use of statistical sampling <u>among</u> the firms as is implied elsewhere. In firm 3, all seniors reporting used the firm's own statistical sampling plan but experienced average sample sizes which were within forty-two line items of firm 6 in which six of seven used judgmental sampling methods (in the latter firm the statistical sampler was the only one of all the statistical samplers who used stratified sampling with optimum allocation). This implies wide variance in statistical sampling skills <u>within</u> some firms.

The use of statistical sampling by the auditor had a significant impact on sample sizes with judgment samples averaging 153.6 while statistical samples averaged 278.6. This result is in conflict with most previously published results[31] and does not, by itself, indicate that judgmental sampling is either superior or inferior to statistical sampling. Such determinations require testing over various accounts, internal control conditions and δ.[32] However, the results do indicate that statistical sampling is not always superior, at least when applied by practicing auditors.

In attempting to determine the extent to which the observed result is due to the implementation of statistical methods by the (practicing) auditor, it is interesting to consider the potential use of stratified methods. Specifically consider a stratified sampling plan based on product type and a Neyman (optimum) allocation between the two types. If seniors in firm 3 (whose seniors followed the firm's own undisclosed statistical sampling plan) and the single statistical sampler from firm 6 who followed a stratified plan with optimum allocation (but with relatively large α, β and E) are excluded, then the average sample size among those using statistical methods in the remaining three firms is 470.2. This implies a standard error which when substituted into the appropriate stratified sampling formula[33] yields a required sample size of 148 which is approximately equal to that of the judgmental group average of 153.6.

Summary

The purpose of this study was to describe extant auditor behavior with respect to a particular audit context. Specifically, ex ante sample sizes were considered as a function of three independent variable groups: 1) level of experience in the use of statistical sampling of the auditor, 2) the firm of the auditor and 3) the sampling method(s) used by the auditor.

Based on the tests conducted, significant differences do exist among firms--perhaps due to differences in basic audit philosophy/technology. This is especially apparent at the statistical sampling level. Also, statistical sampling as currently applied by audit seniors of national CPA firms may not yield smaller sample sizes than judgmental sampling (at least over certain δ and certain accounts). This evidence places in question the apparent historical belief that the employment of statistically-based sampling procedures in the practice of auditing would generate efficiencies over judgmental sampling through the reduction of sample sizes required to meet professional standards. Application of protective sampling did not produce significantly different sample sizes from those of non-protective samplers. Finally, stratified sampling as applied by the seniors did not produce significantly smaller sample sizes.

Extentions of the present work which are likely to be beneficial include: replication over different δ, accounts, population sizes and internal control conditions as well as more precise measurement of the experience/skill variable. Such extentions will allow determination of the conditions under which statistical methods are likely to be beneficial and may reveal a need to improve education levels with respect to statistical sampling.

Figure 1
Analysis of Variance

Source	df	Mean Square	F
Firm	5	107,480	8.65
Method (judgmental, statistical)	1	405,630	32.68
Residual	43	12,411	

Figure 2
Estimated and Actual Sample Sizes
and
Number of Seniors

Firm		Judgment	Statistical	Total
1	Estimated	100.6	352.9	
	Actual	103.7	342	156.7
	Number	7	2	9
2	Estimated	194.2	0	
	Actual	194.2	0	194.3
	Number	8	0	8
3	Estimated	0	82.8	
	Actual	0	82.8	82.8
	Number	0	9	9
4	Estimated	195.4	447.8	
	Actual	163.2	488.0	307.6
	Number	5	4	9
5	Estimated	243.8	496.2	
	Actual	216.7	516.5	388.0
	Number	3	4	7
6	Estimated	92.8	345.2	
	Actual	124.3	125.0	124.4
	Number	7	1	8
Total		153.9	278.6	203.8
		30	20	50

153

Footnotes

[1] The Accountants' Index (published bi-annually by the American Institute of Certified Public Accountants, New York) lists 15 articles published on Sampling during 1971 and 16 during 1972 (supplements 19 and 20).

[2] Statistical sampling herein refers to a sampling plan in which σ is objectively considered in deriving the plan. Judgment sampling refers to all other sampling.

[3] Kenneth W. Stringer, "Practical Aspects of Statistical Sampling in Auditing," 1963 Proceedings of the Business and Economic Statistics Section, American Statistical Association, p. 405; Howard F. Stettler, "Some Observations on Statistical Sampling in Auditing," The Journal of Accountancy April, 1966, pp. 55-60; Robert K. Elliott and John R. Rogers, "Relating Statistical Sampling to Audit Objectives," The Journal of Accountancy, July 1972, pp. 46-55; Robert S. Kaplan, "Statistical Sampling in Auditing with Auxiliary Information Estimators," Report 7314, Center for Mathematical Studies in Business and Economics, University of Chicago, March 1973.

[4] William H. Kraft, Jr., "Statistical Sampling for Auditors: A New Look," The Journal of Accountancy, August 1968, p. 49-56; John A. Tracy, "Bayesian Statistical Methods in Auditing," The Accounting Review, January 1969, p. 90; James E. Sorensen, "Bayesian Analysis in Auditing," The Accounting Review, July 1969, pp. 555-561; Kenneth A. Smith, "The Relationship of Internal Control Evaluation and Audit Sample Size," The Accounting Review, April 1972, pp. 260-269; John C. Corless, "Assessing Prior Distributions for Applying Bayesian Statistics in Auditing," The Accounting Review, July 1972, pp. 556-566.

[5] R. Wayne Stoker, "Using Statistics in Auditing," Selected Papers 1971 Haskins & Sells, (Haskins & Sells: 1972), p. 134 and 140; John Jacobs, "Statistical Sampling - Is it Being Utilized?", The California CPA Quarterly, March, 1971, p. 12; R. K. Metcalf, "Some Applications of Statistical Sampling to Auditing," The Canadian Chartered Accountant, January 1965, p. 36 R. Gene Brown, "Statistical Sampling Tables for Auditors," The Journal of Accountancy, May, 1961, pp. 49-51.

[6] Hamdi F. Aly and Jack I. Duboff, "Statistical vs. Judgmental Sampling: An Empirical Study of Auditing the Accounts Receivable of a Small Retail Store," The Accounting Review, January, 1971, pp. 119-128.

[7] Meigs, Walter B., E. John Larsen and Robert Meigs, Principles of Auditing (fifth edition). (Richard D. Irwin, Inc: 1973), p. 268.

Footnotes (continued)

[8] Two recent studies report on surveys of the extent of use and factors related to the extent of use of statistical sampling by practicing CPAs. (Jacobs, op. cit.; and Timothy Ross, Hugh Hoyt and Herb Shaw, "The Use of Statistical Sampling in Auditing - An Empirical Study", The Ohio CPA, Winter 1972, pp. 5-14). Their results will be compared/contrasted with our own.

[9] Statement on Auditing Standards, American Institute of Certified Public Accountants, 1973, sections 320.70, p. 34.

[10] Other ways of reducing n include the use of other information about the structure of the system being examined such as stratification and/or the use of non-mean-value per unit methods.

[11] A more complete formulation would be expected cost of Type I and Type II errors given that the errors have occurred" since the occurance of an error does not invariably lead to losses. In judgmental sampling the "measures" of α and β are subjective while for statistical sampling α and β can be objectively determined. This may be the primary difference between the two methods.

[12] See Yuji Ijiri and R. S. Kaplan, "A Model for Integrating Sampling Ojbectives in Auditing," Journal of Accounting Research, Spring, 1971, pp. 74-79, concerning the "protective" objective of auditors.

[13] See Kaplan (1973); Cochran, William G., Sampling Techniques, second edition, (John Wiley & Sons, Inc.: 1963) Chapter 6; "Ratio and Difference Estimation," Vol. 5 of An Auditor's Approach to Statistical Sampling, (American Institute of Certified Public Accountants: 1972).

[14] Ross, Hoyt and Shaw, op. cit. p. 11-12.

[15] Brian P. Boas, "A Sample of Statistics", Management Adviser, May-June, 1973, p. 50; Robert L. Grinaker, "Sampling Techniques Related to Audit Objectives", The Illinois CPA, Autumn, 1963, P. 18; Jacobs, op. cit. p. 16.

[16] Jacobs, ibid. p. 14 - 15.

[17] Fred Neumann, "The Auditing Standard of Consistency", Empirical Research in Accounting: Selected Studies, 1968, (Supplement to Vol. 6 of The Journal of Accounting Research); pp. 1-17; and Martin L. Gosman, "Characteristics of Firms Making Accounting Changes", The Journal of Accounting Research, January, 1973, pp. 1-11.

[18] See footnotes 5, 6 and 7 above.

[19] Aly and Duboff, op. cit.

Footnotes (continued)

[20] While previous authors have not necessarily claimed that statistical methods are superior in all individual cases, neither have they indicated conditions under which the opposite is likely to be true.

[21] Cochran, op. cit. p. 99-100.

[22] Ijiri and Kaplan, op. cit.

[23] All 8 firms were contacted but seniors from 2 firms did not respond in numbers sufficient for analysis.

[24] Ross, Hoyt and Shaw, op. cit. p. 9.

[25] However, see Kaplan, op. cit. for some caveats concerning the use of ratio and difference estimates in low error rate populations.

[26] Employees of Big 8 firms in the Ross, Hoyt, Shaw survey, (op. cit., pp 8-10) indicated greater formal training and overall knowledge of statistical methods than did non-Big 8 firm employees.

[27] Sam M. Woolsey, "Materiality Survey", The Journal of Accountancy, (Professional Notes), September 1973, pp. 19-92.

[28] Elliott and Rogers, op. cit., p. 49.

[29] No other interaction effects were tested due to the small number of observations for some combinations.

[30] The hypothesis of independence of experience with statistical sampling and choice of statistical method could not be rejected at even the .5 level.

[31] One study (Jerry W. Kolb, "Statistical Sampling in Auditing," Illinois CPA, Autumn, 1968, pp. 24-28), reports no consistent advantage to either judgment or statistical methods.

[32] Unfortunately, Aly and Duboff, (op. cit.) do not indicate the δ used in their study.

[33] Specifically, the sample size (Y_{opt}) is:

$$Y_{opt} = (\Sigma\ N_k\ \sigma_k)^2\ /\ (V - \Sigma\ N_k\ \sigma_k^2)$$

where V is the desired standard error of the mean and N_k, σ_k are the number of items and standard deviations in each stratum (Cochran, op. cit., p. 97).

By R. Gene Brown

Objective Internal Control Evaluation

*Use of a quantified questionnaire to evalu-
ate the degree of effectiveness of internal
controls is proposed, with examples of how
such a questionnaire might be constructed.*

IT would be difficult to overstate the importance
of the review and appraisal of internal control
by the public accountant and its use as the very
foundation and justification for a program of testing and sampling.[1]

Questionnaires, flow charts, and procedural
work sheets are the tools most commonly used in
this review. Regardless of the *method* employed to
evaluate internal controls, the primary *objective* is
the same: to assist in determining economically and
effectively the extent of testing necessary.

To this end, the auditor *measures* the degree of
effectiveness of internal control which exists. He
does not ascertain the existence or absence of internal control. The results of the measurement are
relative and are subjectively stated, e.g., excellent,
very good, poor. The auditor's opinion with regard
to the adequacy or inadequacy of internal controls forms the foundation for any initial plan for
testing.

Unfortunately, at least three problems arise in
practice as a result of this subjective evaluation of
internal controls. First, several auditors might judge
the effectiveness of a given system of internal con-

trol quite differently. Because of different personal
standards, what is satisfactory to one auditor might
be unsatisfactory to another. This condition devel-
ops primarily from the use of different methods of
appraisal, but can also arise because auditors place
different emphasis on the relative importance of
various factors of internal control.

The second major problem stems from the nature
of the evaluation mechanism itself. Because appraisal is time-consuming, it is a great temptation
to rush through the survey and not accord it the
importance it deserves. Equally tempting is the
possibility of postponing the preparation of the
survey until the "real" auditing is completed.
These problems are complicated by the fact that
most techniques for evaluation are uninteresting
and are a burden on the auditor's client as well as
on the auditor.

A third problem is the difficulty in judging the
over-all effectiveness of internal controls within
individual areas of audit attention—a problem in-
tensified by the breadth of the work required in
appraising the controls, and by the complex interrelationships among various accounts.[2]

Questionnaire offers five advantages

A practical tool is needed to help the auditor
solve these practical problems. It is suggested
that one way of ameliorating this situation is to use
a quantified internal control questionnaire.

The questionnaire is chosen over the flow chart,

---

[1] Saul Levy, "Internal Control and Legal Responsibility,"
THE JOURNAL OF ACCOUNTANCY, February 1957, p. 29.

[2] The questionnaire illustrated in *Montgomery's Auditing*,
8th Ed., contains 917 questions to be answered.

50

procedural work sheets, and other evaluation mechanisms for the following reasons:

1. It permits the use of a standardized approach and working papers prepared in advance.

2. It is faster and more efficient to use.

3. System weaknesses are more obviously isolated for audit attention.

4. It can be used by less highly trained audit personnel.

5. Most important of all, it provides a standard against which to measure existing internal controls—a feature noticeably lacking in other techniques.

Measurement implies some sort of yardstick against which an attribute can be compared. The internal control questionnaire is an attempt to construct such a yardstick, but unfortunately it can be likened to a yardstick with no printed scale. Without intermediate markings, the measurement process is crude at best.

The measurement process has been described as follows:

> The first stage in the development of a full-fledged operational definition of a scientific quality is an intuitive feeling for the quality. The second stage is the discovery of a method of comparison so that it can be said that A has more of the quality in question than B. The third stage is the establishment of a set of standards, which thereby provide categories to which values of the quality can be assigned by means of the comparison test. The fourth step requires a scheme for the interrelation of the standards.[3]

At present, internal control appraisal is at the end of step two of a measuring process. It is now logical and desirable to consider progressing toward step three, the assigning of values. A quantified

<hr />

[3]E. B. Wilson, Jr., *An Introduction to Scientific Research,* New York, McGraw-Hill Book Company, Inc., 1952, p.164.

<hr />

R. GENE BROWN, *Ph.D., CPA, is an assistant professor in the Graduate School of Business Administration, Harvard University. He is a member of the Institute's committee on statistical sampling, and a contributing editor to* THE JOURNAL'*s Education and Professional Training department. He is coauthor of* Sampling Tables for Estimating Error Rates, *published by the University of California (Berkeley) and wrote "Statistical Sampling Tables for Auditors" which appeared in the May 1961* JOURNAL.

internal control questionnaire is one method by which this can be done.[4] Basically, the idea of a quantified questionnaire can be stated as follows:

1. A questionnaire for internal control appraisal for any given audit can be so designed as to represent a conceptually perfect (or wholly satisfactory) system. It can and should include all questions relative to internal accounting controls which might affect the fairness of financial data generated by the system.

2. Within the questionnaire, certain questions are more significant than others; that is, the absence of adequate control is more significant in certain areas than in others.

3. Since certain questions are of greater significance than others, the auditor must decide, judiciously, upon the materiality of the various questions. Since the auditor goes through this thought process anyway, why not attempt to formalize it?

4. This decision, this ranking of questions in terms of materiality, demonstrates that it should be possible to assign numerical values to the questions.

5. Such numerical weights would provide a basis for an objective measurement of the degree of adherence of the particular internal control system to the conceptually perfect (or wholly satisfactory) system visualized by the questionnaire.

Basis for assigning values

A difficult problem in the quantification of the internal control survey is determining the value to be assigned to each question. As mentioned above, some questions are obviously more significant than others. Concerning internal controls in the cash area, for example, the auditor will usually consider it serious if bank balances are not reconciled periodically. On the other hand, he will find it less disturbing if petty cash vouchers are not approved prior to disbursement and/or replenishment. Reconciliation of bank balances and approval of petty cash disbursements are both recognized as elements of a complete internal control system, but the opportunities for defalcation or material misstatement of reported financial data are much more serious in the former case.

Such reasoning exemplifies the value judgment necessary at present in evaluating internal controls.

<hr />

[4]Quantified questionnaires have been used in the social sciences for years, e.g., sociology.

Since reconciliation of cash is very important, a weakness in this area would lead the auditor to extend his normal tests and even change their timing. He probably would not do so because of non-approval of petty cash vouchers; perhaps he would do no more than comment to management that approval prior to disbursement is a sound element of internal control.

Since there is such a difference in materiality between these two elements of internal control in the cash area, it should be possible to recognize this difference by some given quantitative rating scale. The range of such a scale is not significant to the argument. It could be 1 to 5, 1 to 10, or even 1 to 100. In any such scale the high numbers would correspond to the more material items. Certain arguments seem to favor a small range of values for the scale. A primary consideration should be the relative degree of uniformity involved in the decision as to a particular value and the high degree of conformity which would result.

In reference to the cash examples above, and assuming a scale with a range of values from 1 to 5, few auditors would disagree with a weighting of 4 or 5 for the cash reconciliation and 1 for petty cash approvals. The basis for the weighting of each question in the internal control survey is the judgment of the auditor.

The initial reaction to this statement might be that, since the auditor is using his judgment to assign the values, any objectivity in approach is lost. Nothing could be further from the truth! Although judgment can never be removed from the audit process, it can be refined. There is no such thing as an exact, applied science. Only in the abstract can science be exact. The minute an abstract model is adapted to a real-life situation, it becomes inexact. The fact that the input values are subjectively derived does not mean that the quantified internal control questionnaire is unscientific. The initial data of all applied sciences are furnished by qualitative description.[5] The quantified internal control survey provides an objective means for the review and appraisal of internal controls.

To quantify the internal control questionnaire, the auditor must decide upon a range of values to be used, evaluate the materiality of each question in the survey, and assign the proper weight to each question. For purposes of the example outlined herein, the rating scale of 1 to 5 was used. The exhibits at the end of the article illustrate how this process can be accomplished.

Inspection of the questionnaire page will reveal that the only change from the way questionnaires are customarily used involves the two vertical columns at the left-hand side of the page. These columns usually read "yes" and "no." In the example, they are titled "Assigned Value" and "Result of Test." The assigned value is the materiality rating determined for each question. Question 8 (c), Exhibit A, is deemed to be relatively insignificant and so carries an assigned value of one. Formerly the auditor would place a check mark in the appropriate "yes" or "no" column. If the answer to the question is affirmative in the quantified questionnaire, the appropriate point value is entered in the "Result of Test" column. If tests reveal that the response to a particular question is negative, a zero is placed in this column. Within the method described in this article, the answer must be yes or no; hence the numerical value must be either the total assigned or zero. The questions in this particular questionnaire are so written as to preclude partial credit.

Determining control effectiveness by area

Following the completion of questions for a given area of audit attention, the values placed in the "Result of Test" column are totaled. This total provides the basis for determining the over-all internal control effectiveness for the pertinent area. The total is then measured against the total possible for the given area and stated as an "effectiveness index," whose derivation can be expressed as follows:

$$\text{Effectiveness Index} = 100 \left[\frac{\text{Sum of the actual values resulting from testing}}{\text{Sum of the potential values for that audit area}} \right]$$

The computation of the internal control effectiveness index for a specific example can be illustrated as follows: Assume that the total possible points in the area of cash (reflecting the conceptually perfect or wholly satisfactory system envisioned by the questionnaire) amount to 127. A total of 111 points is earned by virtue of affirmative responses to the questionnaire. Thus,

$$\text{E.I.} = 100 \left[\frac{111}{127} \right]$$
$$= 100 \ [0.888]$$
$$= 89\%$$

The auditor now has a quantitative statement of internal control effectiveness for this area, and can

[5] Dagobert D. Runes, *Twentieth Century Philosophy*, New York, Philosophical Library, 1947, p. 112.

159

use it rationally and precisely to determine the extent of testing required in relation to cash.

Using the tools presently available in auditing, the auditor has no truly objective means of measuring internal control effectiveness; he must rely solely on "yes" and "no" answers. The use of a quantified internal control survey retains the advantages of "yes" and "no" answers, but indicates the affirmative response with a numerical value and the negative with a zero. The revised questionnaire gives the auditor more than he now has without removing any of the present advantages.

Other benefits of quantified survey

Some of the advantages of the quantified internal control survey have already been mentioned, but the list of significant benefits is summarized below:

1. It removes nothing from the auditor's techniques for evaluating internal controls; rather, it extends and strengthens them.

2. It gives the auditor an over-all quantitative measure of internal control effectiveness for each area of audit attention.

3. The quantitative measure brings a new objectivity to the statement of results. Assuming that national, intrafirm, or individual audit standards can be set for minimum internal control acceptability, the auditor can more easily measure a particular system against such standards.

4. It will permit the auditor to make a valid trend analysis on recurring engagements. A year-by-year improvement in internal control effectiveness would show up distinctly in the ratings. For example, if the effectiveness index were 78 per cent in 1958, 82 per cent in 1959, 84 per cent in 1960 and 91 per cent in 1961, the auditor could justifiably consider adjusting his amount of testing. At present, since improvements in internal control are not so obvious, the testing levels of prior years are occasionally maintained for some time until improvements become clearly recognizable.

5. The conclusions of the auditor relative to internal controls will be more easily demonstrable to other interested persons. As a result, the quality of work can be more easily controlled, within both the profession and the firm. Since the index summarizes the results for the auditor, he is not forced to attempt a subjective evaluation involving many complex and interrelated questions which in aggregate practically defy precise verbal description.

6. The internal control effectiveness index will assist in the effective implementation of statistical sampling. Because of the inexactness of present internal control measurement techniques, attempts to apply statistical sampling have been little more than abstractions of a conceptually precise tool. Since the degree of confidence (risk) and/or the level of accuracy required for statistical sampling are based on the evaluation of internal controls, these decisions can be more easily made if an objective measurement of internal controls is available.

7. It should remove some of the drudgery from the auditors' preparation and subsequent review of the questionnaire. The prospect of determining numerical ratings of the various facets of internal control would certainly warrant the increased attention and interest of both the auditor and the management of the firm subject to examination.

Possible arguments or objections

Aside from the natural human resistance to change, there are several objections which might arise regarding a quantified internal control questionnaire.

Probably the first and immediate objection would be that the auditor's judgment is being superseded or impeded. Any such argument is unsound. To do his job effectively, the auditor must be equipped with both technical proficiency and good judgment. The quantification of the internal control survey adds to his technical tools, but not at the expense of his judgment. It must be remembered that the input values are still derived judiciously. The results of the internal control survey help the auditor choose the appropriate risk and desired accuracy for subsequent testing; he can do so more easily because there is a more precise statement of the degree of effectiveness of internal control.

A second objection might be that the proposed quantification is too mechanical. However, it is no more mechanical than the present questionnaire. Instead of checkmarks, the auditor places numerical values in the appropriate columns. Any approach to surveying internal controls that provides for an affirmative or negative response is bound to be somewhat mechanical. Even though the tool that provides the auditor with information about the status of internal controls tends to be mechanical, the evaluation and utilization of the results are not. The auditor will still use the questionnaire results in the manner judged most appropriate for the particular audit.

A third major criticism might be that question-weighting is of dubious value, particularly since it is impossible to weight the various questions accurately. All questions are important, so the argument might run, or they would not be included in the questionnaire. To argue in this manner denies the fact that the questions have varying significance in their relation to the amount of testing to be done. It should be obvious to the experienced auditor that many questions are extremely material, while others may be necessary to internal controls but are considerably less important in their potential effect on audit testing. Probably the real source of any dissatisfaction with question-weighting is the obvious uncertainty over what values to assign rather than whether weighting is conceptually worthwhile. It is true, of course, that equally experienced auditors might assign different values to a given question during their initial experience with this method. Certain individual weights assigned to the internal control survey illustrated in Exhibits A and B might well be questioned in certain respects. However, this should not cause immediate concern. The primary argument for the moment is that the internal control questionnaire can and should be quantified. The latitude and uncertainty in assigning weights will significantly decrease as familiarity with the technique is acquired.

Judgment, experience are required

Any new product can be improved. The primary source of information for determining final questionnaire values (if it is really desirable to do so) will result from a considerable distillation of audit experience. Initially, the flexibility in values that could be assigned provides the necessary means for implementing diversity in audit judgment. It is questionable whether such diversity should (or would) continue unresolved for any length of time. However, in the interest of promoting new ideas and techniques, it must be tolerated temporarily. To hand the quantified questionnaire to an experienced auditor without permitting him to participate in the process of assigning values is tantamount to accepting failure prior to trial. It is possible, of course, that someday it may be possible to set rather specific national auditing standards. However, due to the current state of the art, this is not a feasible short-term objective.

The fourth criticism which might be voiced is that the use of a standardized questionnaire, which is relatively common, would not lend itself to quantification. This is because certain weaknesses are more important in some engagements than in others. However, certain arguments seem to favor a standard questionnaire. The major one is that even though the emphasis on the various sections of the questionnaire might vary with each engagement, the particular questions within each area of audit attention are of the same relative importance. For example, emphasis on the cash portion of an audit would be much more significant for a retail outlet than for a branch manufacturing plant. Nevertheless, monthly cash reconciliation is equally important for both. The emphasis on the cash portion of the audit will vary between the two jobs; but within each section of the questionnaire, the relative importance of each question would be roughly the same. In essence, this is one of the peculiar advantages of the quantified questionnaire; even though the same techniques of analysis are used, the results of the particular analysis provide sufficient flexibility for use in almost all audit engagements. Whether it is possible to construct a questionnaire applicable to most engagements remains to be seen, but the successful use of many standardized audit programs suggests that it is.

A final possible criticism is that the use of an over-all rating for each area obscures the significance of individual questions. For example, it is argued that four negative responses for questions weighted one point each is not identical in materiality with one negative response for a four-point question. This argument is sound. The auditor must consider each question as well as the total effectiveness index. He does this at present and should continue to peruse the responses to the individual questions. There are two reasons for assigning values to individual questions in the questionnaire. The first, as previously mentioned, is to permit a summary statement in quantitative terms about internal control effectiveness for an individual area of audit concentration. The second objective is to give an indication of the relative importance of *each question*. The intent is not to shift the emphasis in evaluating internal control from specific problem areas to a general over-all evaluation. The computation of the internal control effectiveness index does not eliminate the necessity of considering the answer to each question in the survey. The analysis by area of audit attention permits an overview of the complex interrelationships of internal controls, while the perusal of individual questions permits the auditor to plan his testing in detail. In addition, the numerical values assigned to each question will assist the inexperienced auditor in picturing the significance of negative responses.

Questionnaire is not the final answer

It is felt that suggested limitations or disadvantages of the quantified questionnaire are relatively insignificant when compared with its advantages.

It should be pointed out that the main thesis of

161

this article is that serious consideration should be given to developing more objective methods for evaluating internal control. The questionnaire method was selected because at first glance it seems to be a way of doing so within the framework of present techniques. It is not implied that all auditors do or should use a questionnaire in evaluating internal control. In fact, due to the increasing importance of that preliminary phase of the audit dealing with the internal control appraisal, it is quite likely that several different techniques will be used in the future. It is hoped that one or more of them will be so constructed as to yield a *quantitative* statement of internal control reliability.

Exhibit A[6]
General
Part I—Internal Accounting Control

Assigned Value	Result of Test	
		1. Is a chart of accounts in use? (A formal chart of accounts is a list of accounts, systematically arranged, indicating account names and numbers.)
5		
3		2. Is the chart of accounts supplemented by definitions of items to be recorded in the various accounts? (The definitions of items to be included in the accounts promote consistency in recording and summarizing accounting transactions.)
5		3. Is an accounting manual in use? (Such a manual should prescribe procedures to be followed in recording and summarizing accounting transactions.)
2		4. Is the assignment of accounting duties and responsibilities expressed in the form or an organization chart? (Such a chart is a formal expression of assignments, showing functional responsibilities; these assignments may also be expressed in the form of job descriptions.)
5		5. Are all postings to general and subsidiary ledgers required to be supported by entries in books of original entry or journal entries?
5		6. Are ledger entries clearly referenced to indicate their source?
		7. Are journal entries:
5		(a) Standardized for content and identification?
5		(b) Supported by readily identifiable data?
3		(c) Reviewed and approved by a responsible employee?
		8. Are the original recording and summarizations of accounting transactions reviewed to assure adherence to:
2		(a) Chart of accounts?
2		(b) Accounting manual instructions?
1		(c) Assignments indicated by the organization chart? (These reviews may be made by department heads, the chief accounting officer, or other assigned personnel. When a formal chart of accounts, accounting manual, or organization chart is not in use, a file of instructions may contain equivalent data.)

[6]Norman J. Lenhart and Philip L. Defliese, *Montgomery's Auditing*, New York, Ronald Press, 1957, pp. 643 for Exhibit A and 668 for Exhibit B. The two pages from the questionnaire in *Montgomery's Auditing* have been reproduced by permission of the copyright holder and publisher, Ronald Press. The two columns headed "Assigned Value" and "Result of Test" and the numerical values were added by this writer and do not appear in the book.

Assigned Value	Result of Test	

Accounts receivable:

21. Are statements of accounts regularly sent to *all* customers?

3
    (Periodic statements provide opportunities for debtors to report differences. If it is not the practice to send statements regularly to all customers, objectives might be partially attained by other means. For example:

    (a) Statements might be mailed only to customers with delinquent balances.

    (b) A delinquent notice to an installment or budget account customer when payments are not received as due is a form of statement to the customer.

    (c) Bills from public utilities and other companies furnishing services may serve the dual purpose of invoice and statement.)

22. Are credit memorandums for returned merchandise, price adjustments, special discounts, and damage claims:

5
    (a) Under numerical control?

2
    (b) Issued promptly on receipt of proper authorization?

4
    (c) Recorded promptly when issued?

2
    (d) Approved by a responsible person?

    (Undue delay in recording these credits may result in a substantial overstatement of accounts receivable.)

23. Are aging schedules:

3
    (a) Prepared periodically?

1
    (b) Reviewed by a responsible person?

    (The review should include consideration of the amount of allowance to be provided for doubtful accounts.)

24. Is approval of a responsible person required for:

5
    (a) Payment of customer credit balances?

2
    (b) Write-off of uncollectible amounts?

25. Are accounts receivable that have been written off:

5
    (a) Under accounting control?

2
    (b) Reviewed periodically by an informed person?

    (Frequently these accounts are transferred to a bad debt ledger under memorandum control.)

List of Titles

Accounting History and the Development of a Profession

Management Accounting Research: A Review and Annotated Bibliography.
Charles F. Klemstine and Michael W. Maher. New York, 1984.

Accounting Literature in Non-Accounting Journals: An Annotated Bibliography.
Panadda Tantral. New York, 1984.

The Evolution of Behavioral Accounting Research: An Overview.
Robert H. Ashton, editor. New York, 1984.

Some Early Contributions to the Study of Audit Judgment.
Robert H. Ashton, editor. New York, 1984.

Depreciation and Capital Maintenance.
Richard P. Brief, editor. New York, 1984.

The Case for Continuously Contemporary Accounting.
G. W. Dean and M. C. Wells, editors. New York, 1984.

Studies of Company Records: 1830–1974.
J. R. Edwards, editor. New York, 1984.

European Equity Markets: Risk, Return, and Efficiency.
Gabriel Hawawini and Pierre Michel, editors. New York, 1984.

Transactions of the Chartered Accountants Students' Societies of Edinburgh and Glasgow: A Selection of Writings, 1886–1958.
Thomas A. Lee, editor. New York, 1984.

The Development of Double Entry: Selected Essays.
Christopher Nobes, editor. New York, 1984.

Papers on Accounting History.
R. H. Parker. New York, 1984.

Collected Papers on Accounting and Accounting Education.
David Solomons. New York, 1984.

The General Principles of the Science of Accounts and the Accountancy of Investment.
Charles E. Sprague. New York, 1984.

Selected Papers on Accounting, Auditing, and Professional Problems.
Edward Stamp. New York, 1984.

Factory Accounts.
John Whitmore. New York, 1984.

Sourcebook on Accounting Principles and Auditing Procedures: 1917–1953 (in two volumes).
Stephen A. Zeff and Maurice Moonitz, editors. New York, 1984.

The First Fifty Years 1913–1963.
Arthur Andersen Company. Chicago, 1963.

Paciolo on Accounting.
R. Gene Brown and Kenneth S. Johnston. New York, 1963.

The Early History of Coopers & Lybrand.
Coopers & Lybrand. New York, 1984.

Report of the Trial . . . Against the Directors and the Manager of the City of Glasgow Bank.
Charles Tennant Couper. Edinburgh, 1879.

Development of Accounting Thought.
Harvey T. Deinzer. New York, 1965.

The Principles of Auditing.
F.R.M. De Paula. London, 1915.

The Accountant, or, the Method of Bookkeeping Deduced from Clear Principles, and Illustrated by a Variety of Examples.
James Dodson. London, 1750.

A Common Sense Method of Double Entry Bookkeeping, on First Principles, as Suggested by De Morgan. Part I, Theoretical.
S. Dyer. London, 1897.

Economics of Fatigue and Unrest and the Efficiency of Labour in English and American Industry.
P. Sargant Florence. London, 1923.

Haskins & Sells: Our First Seventy-Five Years.
Arthur B. Foye. New York, 1970.

The History of the Society of Incorporated Accountants, 1885–1957.
A. A. Garrett. Oxford, 1961.

The Game of Budget Control.
Geert Hofstede. Assen, 1967.

The History of The Institute of Chartered Accountants in England and Wales 1880–1965, and of Its Founder Accountancy Bodies 1870–1880.
Sir Harold Howitt. London, 1966.

History of the Chartered Accountants of Scotland from the Earliest Times to 1954.
Institute of Chartered Accountants of Scotland. Edinburgh, 1954.

Accounting Thought and Education: Six English Pioneers.
J. Kitchen and R. H. Parker. London, 1980.

The Evolution of Corporate Financial Reporting.
T. A. Lee and R. H. Parker. Middlesex, 1979.

Accounting in Scotland: A Historical Bibliography.
Janet E. Pryce-Jones and R. H. Parker. Edinburgh, 1976.

A History of Accountants in Ireland.
H. W. Robinson. Dublin, 1964.

The Sixth International Congress on Accounting.
London, 1952.

The Accomptant's Oracle: or, Key to Science, Being a Compleat Practical System of Book-keeping.
Wardbaugh Thompson. York, 1777.

Accountancy in Transition

The Tangled Web of Price Variation Accounting: The Development of Ideas Underlying Professional Prescriptions in Six Countries.
F. L. Clarke. New York, 1982.

Beta Alpha Psi, From Alpha to Omega: Pursuing a Vision of Professional Education for Accountants, 1919–1945.
Terry K. Sheldahl. New York, 1982.

Four Classics on the Theory of Double-Entry Bookkeeping.
Richard P. Brief, editor. New York, 1982.

Forerunners of Realizable Values Accounting in Financial Reporting.
G. W. Dean and M. C. Wells, editors. New York, 1982.

Accounting Queries.
Harold C. Edey. New York, 1982.

The Development of Accounting Theory: Significant Contributors to Accounting Thought in the 20th Century.
Michael Gaffikin and Michael Aitken, editors. New York, 1982.

Studies in Social and Private Accounting.
Solomon Fabricant. New York, 1982.

Bond Duration and Immunization: Early Developments and Recent Contributions.
Gabriel A. Hawawini, editor. New York, 1982.

Further Essays on the History of Accounting.
Basil S. Yamey. New York, 1982.

Accounting Principles Through The Years: The Views of Professional and Academic Leaders 1938–1954.
Stephen A. Zeff, editor. New York, 1982.

The Accounting Postulates and Principles Controversy of the 1960s.
Stephen A. Zeff, editor. New York, 1982.

Fiftieth Anniversary Celebration.
American Institute of Accountants. New York, 1937.

Library Catalogue.
American Institute of Accountants. New York, 1919.

Four Essays in Accounting Theory.
F. Sewell Bray. London, 1953. *bound with*
Some Accounting Terms and Concepts.
Institute of Chartered Accountants in England and Wales and The National Institute of Economic and Social Research. Cambridge, 1951.

Accounting in Disarray.
R. J. Chambers. Melbourne, 1973.

The Balance-Sheet.
Charles B. Couchman. New York, 1924.

Audits.
Arthur E. Cutforth. London, 1906.

Methods of Amalgamation.
Arthur E. Cutforth. London, 1926.

Deloitte & Co. 1845–1956.
Sir Russell Kettle. Oxford, 1958. *bound with*
Fifty-seven Years in an Accountant's Office.
Ernest Cooper. London, 1921.

Accountants and the Law of Negligence.
R. W. Dickerson. Toronto, 1966.

Consolidated Statements.
H. A. Finney. New York, 1922.

The Rate of Interest.
Irving Fisher. New York, 1907.

Holding Companies and Their Published Accounts.
Sir Gilbert Garnsey. London, 1923. *bound with*
Limitations of a Balance Sheet.
Sir Gilbert Garnsey. London, 1928.

Accounting Concepts of Profit.
Stephen Gilman. New York, 1939.

*An Introduction to Merchandise, Parts IV and V
(Italian Bookkeeping and Practical Bookkeeping).*
Robert Hamilton. Edinburgh, 1788.

The Merchant's Magazine: or, Trades-man's Treasury.
Edward Hatton. London, 1695.

The Law of Accounting and Financial Statements.
George S. Hills. Boston, 1957.

International Congress on Accounting 1929.
New York, 1930.

Fourth International Congress on Accounting 1933.
London, 1933.

Magnificent Masquerade.
Charles Keats. New York, 1964.

Profit Measurement and Price Changes.
Kenneth Lacey. London, 1952.

The American Accomptant.
Chauncey Lee. Lansingburgh, 1797.

Consolidated Balance Sheets.
George Hills Newlove. New York, 1926.

Consolidated and Other Group Accounts.
T. B. Robson. London, 1950.

Accounting Method.
C. Rufus Rorem. Chicago, 1928.

Shareholder's Money.
Horace B. Samuel. London, 1933.

Standardized Accountancy in Germany. (With a new appendix.)
H. W. Singer. Cambridge, 1943.

*The Securities and Exchange Commission in the Matter of McKesson
& Robbins, Inc. Report on Investigation.*
Washington, D. C., 1940.

*The Securities and Exchange Commission in the Matter of McKesson
& Robbins, Inc. Testimony of Expert Witnesses.*
Washington, D. C., 1939.

Accounting in England and Scotland: 1543–1800.
B. S. Yamey, H. C. Edey, Hugh W. Thomson. London, 1963.